GHOST TRAILS OF NORTHUMBRIA

by

CLIVE KRISTEN

Dedication

To Aidan and Jill Harrison

Published by Casdec Ltd
22 Harraton Terrace
Birtley
Chester-le-Street
Co. Durham
DH3 2QG

Tel: (091) 410 5556
Fax: (091) 410 0229

Written by Clive Kristen

First Published May 1992

ISBN - 0 907595 80 4

Author's Note

Dear Ghosthunter,

This book contains five 'tour and explore' trails linked by supernatural themes.

These trails have been constructed to take best advantage of the great natural beauty of the region, and to bring to life Northumbria's rich historical and cultural heritage.

The 'touring times' suggested for each trail are based on a fairly brisk schedule. For those who prefer relaxed ghosthunting each trail can be conveniently broken down into sections. The third trail, for instance, could be easily extended to take three or four days. The Trail Guides provided with each section are intended only to help make sense of the text. They are not to scale and should not be regarded as an adequate substitute for a good map.

Whist every effort has been made to produce accurate historical and topographical detail, the reader will understand that no area of human consciousness is more prone to misinterpretation, confusion, and even dishonesty than the supernatural.

In an attempt to make sense of this dilemma the book tries to balance traditional accounts of supernatural phenomena, archive and historical material with the common sense of local knowledge. When it has been necessary to select one version of a story from several, contemporary and local accounts have taken precedence.

The historical notes are intended to fill out detail where it has not been appropriate to do so within the main body the the text. This final section also corrects a measure of imbalance. It was impossible to discuss the Bamburgh area without referring in some detail to two great Northumberland heroines - Grace Darling and Dorothy Forster. But Margaret of Anjou is mentioned all too briefly. In many ways she is a more significant historical figure and a most celebrated ghost.

I am indebted to archivists and librarians in Britain and abroad without whose patience and perseverance this would have been a very much slimmer volume. I also extend grateful thanks to my wife, Maureen, for her encouragement, ghosthunting and mapmaking skills. Finally I thank all the people who have given me primary source material for this book by telling their tales of encounters with the supernatural.

Clive Kristen
May 1992

The Writer

Former teacher and lecturer, Clive Kristen, joined the ranks of professional writers three years ago.

He is a contributor to a number of national publications, but is best known locally for copywriting, and as an outspoken freelance news and feature writer for the Northumberland Gazette.

The Photographer

Duncan Elson is well established as one of the region's leading portrait and landscape photographers.

His award winning work has qualified him as a Master Photographer and he is a Licentiate Member of the British Institute of Professional Photographers.

The Illustrator

The cover and map designs show two creative facets in the wide repertoire of Mark Nuttall's skills as an illustrator.

Mark, who is currently working in graphic design for television, is also noted for his distinctive cartoon strips.

CONTENTS

Grizzel's Clump - page 65
'An Improbable Haunting'

Taking Care in the Countryside

Most of the sites in this book can be accessed from public rights of way. Where this does not happen visitors can get a good impression of a site from suggested viewpoints.

Much of the land is farmed, and should be treated with respect. In a few cases, access is restricted and the necessary consents should be obtained. Special care is required during the lambing season and visitors are requested to follow the guidelines of the country code. Please follow footpaths, close gates, and keep dogs under close control. Litter is unsightly and can cause injury and suffering to animals.

Some of the buildings mentioned are private homes. Please do not trespass or behave intrusively. Property owners have been generous in the information they have provided. Please ensure that their right to quiet and privacy is preserved.

These tours are designed for the motorist and none of the walks suggested are arduous. Nevertheless, Northumbrian weather can be unpredictable - even in summer. It is suggested that visitors do not set out on a walk alone. They should have adequate footwear and a waterproof garment. A good map and compass are also highly recommended.

The Author

No.1 - Witches and Wedlock

This circular motoring tour takes about six hours

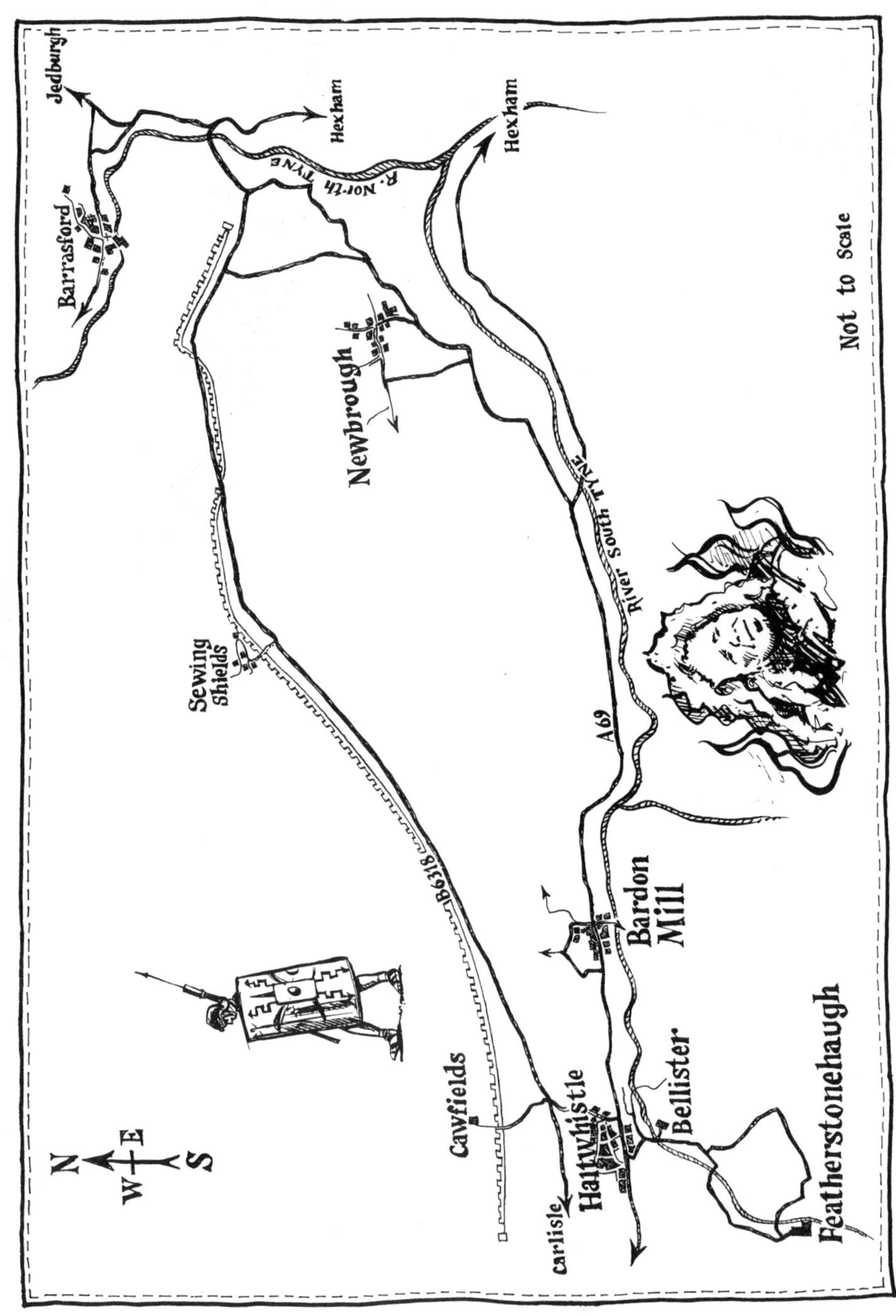
Jedburgh
Hexham
Hexham
Barrasford
R. North Tyne
Newbrough
Not to Scale
Sewing Shields
River South Tyne
A69
B6318
Bardon Mill
Cawfields
Haltwhistle
Bellister
Featherstonehaugh
Carlisle
N
E
W
S

A Sense of History

The valleys of the North and South Tyne are frequently overlooked by visitors. There is almost certainly a result of the proximity of Northumberland's hills and beaches to the north and east, and the well documented attractions of the Lake District and Dales to the south and west.

The valleys tend to be places that visitors pass through on their way to somewhere else, and yet they are missing a great deal. There is much to explore here. The area offers quiet roads and deserted footpaths and unspoilt landscapes of great charm. There are excellent and inexpensive recreational facilities of all kinds, and a welcome sense of tradition and history everywhere.

For the ghost hunter, the area provides a rich mine of supernatural activity.

Barrasford, as the name implies, developed from a crossing place on the North Tyne. It is a tidy, compact village, which provides the best viewing point for Haughton Castle across the river.

The building, which is in private ownership, is impressively set on an elevated site above the wooded river bank. It is essentially a 19th. century reconstruction of an important battlemented castle that was completed in the 15th. century and ruined two hundred years later.

The Terrible Haunting of Sir Thomas de Widdrington

During the reign of Henry VIII the popular Lord of Haughton was Sir Thomas de Widdrington.

Local landowners were angered with the behaviour of a certain Lord Dacre, Warden of the Middle Marches, who was rumoured to be in league with the moss-trooping clans of Liddlesdale. Sir Thomas de Widdrington was entrusted by the landowners to take a petition of these grievances to Cardinal Wolsey at York.

Before leaving on his journey Sir Thomas secured the arrest of Archie Armstrong - chief of a Liddlesdale clan. The arrest was important because Armstrong had particularly close ties with the devious Lord Dacre. One relationship that concerned landowners was that between Lord Dacre and the famously attractive Helen Armstrong, sister to the clan's chief.

When Sir Thomas reached York he found 'attached to his girdle' a key, which he knew to be the only means of opening the deepest dungeon at Haughton Castle.

Realising immediately that Archie Armstrong had already been without food and drink for three days, the worthy Thomas forgot his business with Wolsey and galloped northwards at top speed. One horse dropped dead beneath him near Durham, and a second was exhausted when he arrived at Haughton.

Now close to collapse himself, Sir Thomas went immediately to the dungeons and opened the hatch of the oubliette. The air was filled with 'a wretched malodorous smell' and the torches revealed an 'indescribable look of agony' in the wide-eyed face of the corpse.

The unfortunate man had died in convulsions after gnawing through the flesh of his own arm. Other marks around the wrists suggested that he had also drunk his own blood.

The ghost of Archie Armstrong tormented Sir Thomas as the grisly phantom haunted every inch of the castle and grounds. It appeared in an unoccupied place at the dining table and pointed an accusing finger at Sir Thomas. It appeared in his bedchamber, standing silently at the foot of the bed to greet him with a dreadful grin as he awoke from his sleep. It lurked on the staircase and gave out terrible shrieks and screams as Sir Thomas approached. The most dreadful encounter of all was when the spectre leapt from behind upon the knight's shoulders as he walked in the woods. Sir Thomas never forgot the touch of icy fingers on his neck or the hideous ring of laughter as the restless spirit floated up and away into the canopy of the trees.

The Exorcism

Finally Sir Thomas could live no longer with these daily terrors and a priest was brought from Simonburn to exorcize the 'pitiful spirit'. This was apparently achieved successfully by using a 'black-letter' bible.

In 1861 the bible was removed for repair. Renewed hauntings so distressed the castle's owner that he demanded the immediate return of the book. By tradition all ghostly activity ended immediately, but there have been claims by Barrasford people that 'terrible shrieks and screams' can still be heard wafting over the water from time to time. It is also said that Archie Armstrong's ghost has been seen rising from the water near the ford and floating in the air near to the river's edge. A bloody arm is raised above the phantom's head in a gesture that may be a macabre salute to Sir Thomas de Widdrington.

A Burning Question

Placing a first division phantom at the beginning of the trail could indicate there will be something of a journey before the ghost hunter encounters anything similarly interesting. Barrasford however offers special value in spooky surprises.

The Barrasford Arms Hotel stands on the site of a much earlier coaching inn. The previous establishment was burnt to the ground a little over a century ago and at least one person succumbed to the flames.

On several occasions there have been reports of a man running into the road with his body and clothing a raging inferno of fire. This apparition disappears almost as soon as it is seen, but anguished shouts continue to be heard for some time from the place where the apparition vanishes.

Those who consider that one set of pitiful yells are pretty much like another, may point to possible confusion between the fiery phantom and the ghost of Archie Armstrong. One witness has reported that the hotel's ghost creates a most impressive sound - described as 'a high-pitched staccato cadence of ear-shattering squeals' - which form the dramatic highlight and finale of each unhappy performance. This is very different from the 'terrible shrieks and screams' attributed to the castle phantom which are said to be delivered with 'distinctively pregnant pauses' between one sound and the next.

The Cobbler's Leap

Barrasford's final ghostly phenomenon can be located a couple of hundred yards 'uphill' from the hotel. If the visitor turns down a small lane between the methodist chapel and country store, a building called Rose Cottage (now two houses) can be located near the gate to a farm yard. The 'cottage' has an unusual inner and outer chimney arrangement and there is a broken cartwheel fixed to a wall opposite.

A hundred and fifty years ago Rose Cottage was the home of the village cobbler. Barrasford locals still 'recall' that the cobbler became increasingly deranged until one day he ended his life by leaping from an upstairs window.

Present and previous owners of the 'cottage' claim that it has a 'strange atmosphere' which sometimes makes guests and visitors uncomfortable. Locals talk about the force of 'an unseen presence' in parts of the building.

On a sunny summer's day Rose Cottage looks as pleasing and innocent as its name suggests, and there are no recorded accounts of a haunting. The upper windows are less than twenty feet above ground level and it is even surprising perhaps that the cobbler's fall should have proved fatal.

Old Meg of Newbrough

If Rose Cottage seems an unlikely setting for unpleasant manifestations, the story of Old Meg of Newbrough reaches the outer limits limits of credibility.
The village of Newbrough has Roman origins. It was the site of a fort on the line of the Stanegate - once an important supply road for Hadrian's Wall. There is little here to prove Roman origins, and even a few fine vernacular buildings seem swamped by modern development.

The visitor should take a narrow lane northwards which runs between the Red Lion and the Stanegate Hotel. After passing through a gate the lane becomes a metalled track which rises eventually to some farm buildings. It is recommended that visitors should treat the road from this point as a footpath and walk the two hundred metres or so to a point where the road begins to dip gently downwards.

The views from this point back towards the Tyne valley are delightful. On the left (westwards) there is a patchwork of small conifer plantations. Meggie's Dene flows down from the gently rolling slopes of Torney's Fell.

The Dene takes its name from Old Meg, who was burnt as a witch in the 16th. century.

It seems that the burning took place away from the village to reduce the possibility of her spirit returning to take revenge on her persecutors. As additional insurance a stake was driven through her charred heart before the burial.

It is tricky to find the exact place where this dreadful event happened. Only one real clue is provided. It

Meggie's Dene at Dusk

was recorded that 'the grave is marked by a pink thorn tree that grows by the water's edge'.

Unfortunately the hollows in the field below the road at this point contain thriving mini-coppices of pink thorn trees. Another problem of location is that Meggie's Dene is an inconsequential and frequently dried up stream.

A grassed-over wall is the signpost down to the thorn trees. There are many splendidly gnarled specimens here, and any could be chosen to worthily mark a witch's grave, but the visitor should not be distracted.

At a point below where the main stream meets two smaller becks from the hillside, there are a couple of less impressive, but equally ancient, thorn trees. A pile of stones seems to mark a spot by one of them.

It is not claimed that this is the spot, only that it could be. There is a traditional association between witchcraft and water, and in the mystique of folklore a place where waters joined would be a favoured site to bury a witch.

The story of Old Meg varies much with the teller. Common threads suggest that she was a strange - and probably senile - old woman who managed to upset some of the worthy citizen's of Newbrough. It is also said that she had distinctive yellow canine teeth. Today she would have ended her days in a geriatric ward or an old peoples' home. Those who bemoan the passing of 'the good old days' may wish to consider the alternative solutions that could be applied to social problems only four centuries ago.

Bardon Mill, a bustling semi-industrialised village, provides a marked contrast to the rugged beauty of Meggie's Dene.

The last colliery in West Northumberland (which closed in 1973) was once the core of the local economy. Today Bardon Mill is best known as a communication point for the Northumberland Lakes, and as a thoroughfare to Vindolanda - the second most visited Roman site on Hadrian's Wall.

The village is not without character, and the small Greyhound Inn is reputed to be haunted. If so, the inn's ghostly inhabitant must suffer an identity crisis - he is variously described as a blacksmith, a collier, a poacher and a priest...

At Hardriding Farm (towards Haltwhistle) there is a much better documented ghost.

The Anniversary Ghost

Towards the middle of the fourteenth century a notorious robber was murdered here, most likely for the stolen money he was carrying. The last reported visit of the ghost was in 1933 when mysterious shouts and banging doors awoke the inhabitants of the farm.

There has been some speculation that the ghost restricts his activity to particular anniversaries, and that the centenary of his death is a particularly auspicious time for a haunting. It is possible that the last reported visit marked six centuries exactly since the murder - a hypothesis that cannot be properly tested until 2033.

The small market town of Haltwhistle is disappointing in terms of supernatural phenomena, but it is well worth visiting the ancient Holy Cross Church behind the market-place. There are claims that a church was founded on this site around 1178 by William the Lion, King of Scotland.

An Interesting Church

We can be absolutely sure that this early English parish church was completed by the middle of the 13th. century. The exterior of the building is plain, and unusual in that it has no tower. The nave and aisles are very wide and form an almost perfect square. The chancel and nave (which has a fine painted roof) were once level. Their present varying heights are the result of extensive Victorian 'restoration'.

The church also contains three fine medieval gravestones that date from the middle of the 14th. century. The most interesting is that of a member of the Blenkinsopp family. It bears the family arms, a floreated cross and sword, and a staff and bag indicating that he had once gone on a pilgrimage.

In the south wall of the chancel is a stone slab that commemorates John Ridley, a relative of Bishop Ridley who was burnt at the stake in Oxford in 1555.

The Bellister Gallows Tree

Taking the Alston road out of Haltwhistle, the visitor will cross a single-track bridge and turn right to view the ruins of Bellister Castle. The castle is open to the public by appointment.

A large castellated farmhouse dominates what remains of the castle which was already 'in much decay' when the Blenkinsopp family took it over in the 16th. century. The size of the (partly artificial) mound on which it was built suggests it was once a place of 'considerable extent'. It is likely that the farmhouse occupies the original site of the bailey.

On the south side of the tower is an old tree. One of the branches runs out horizontally and local tradition has it that this made an excellent gallows. It is claimed that seven moss-troopers were once strung up at the same time.

Bellister Castle

The Tale of the Grey Man

Bellister's celebrated ghost is the 'Grey Man'.

The story is that a wandering minstrel called at the tower and was given food and the promise of a bed for the night. For some unknown reason the lord of Bellister became suspicious of the stranger, thinking that he may be an assassin sent by an enemy.

The minstrel became apprehensive as he found the lord's attitude hardening towards him, and he decided to escape rather than retire to his room.

Finding the minstrel had vanished the lord believed that his fears were justified. Guards and dogs were dispatched to find the man. The scent was strong and the dogs caught the minstrel on the slippery river bank. By the time the guards caught up with the dogs the poor minstrel was torn to pieces.

For the rest of his days the baron suffered frequent visits from the ghost of the minstrel. In the best traditions of haunting the apparition was a sickening sight, with blood-stained tattered rags and repulsive jagged open wounds around his neck and face.

In similar style to the ghost of Archie Armstrong at Haughton this phantom would frequently choose inconvenient moments to appear - such as when the family were at dinner or entertaining guests. The unhappy ghost would always point an accusing finger at the baron and loudly proclaim the injustice done to him.

Locals will still tell you that from time to time the sound of baying hounds is heard in the woods beside the Tyne. The chorus of baying mingles in the air with the anguished shrieks of the Grey Man of Bellister.

The Poacher's Tale

Two brothers, Raymond and Ben Nash from Hexham, suffered a spine chilling experience in those same woods in the late 1950's.

" *I won't say what we were doing there,* " *says Raymond,* " *but I do remember that the salmon were running well that night. We were both well used to the dark. Like lots of other lads we reckoned we were frightened of nothing.* "

" *It started with Ben's torch flickering. We couldn't understand it. One minute it was working normally, but then it just turned itself on and off. When my light started doing the same we couldn't believe it. The daft thing was it made no difference if you turned them off or on - they just kept flickering.* "

" Ben heard something in the woods and I reckoned the lights were giving us away. We stuffed them deep into our jackets and just stood there watching. I heard branches cracking. I reckoned it was upstream and signalled to Ben to follow me down with the flow. "

" That's when it happened. They came from nowhere. Hounds of hell I call them. There were four of them - the biggest black brutes you've ever seen. They ran straight at us. The terrible howling froze your blood. The huge teeth would have torn you to rags in no time. I thought I was a dead man. I was screaming and screaming. I threw myself on the ground and covered my face with my arms. "

" But nothing happened. I was waiting to die and nothing happened. I rolled over after a while and peered out one eye through a gap between my arms. There was nothing there. I couldn't believe it. All I could hear was the sound of Ben sobbing. We couldn't stop shivering for ages after, but we never heard or saw them again."

" The worst thing was the smell. It was like piles of rotten fish stuck right under your nose. It made you retch. I was glad to get away from there I can tell you. I've not been back again either."

The Ghostly Wedding Party

Every castle seems to provide a ghost or two. As Northumbria has traditionally been the most heavily fortified corner of England, this must explain why there are such abundant riches for visitors with an interest in the supernatural.

Featherstone Castle is no disappointment.

The road from Bellister enters Park village. Turn first right past the Wallace Arms and the visitor is rewarded with splendid views over the Featherstone battlements and the South Tyne valley.

After passing a lion-crested filled-in gateway it is best to drive beyond the castle and park near the river footbridge. An excellent footpath follows the south side of the river past the castle to some gateposts - once the entrance to a Prisoner of War camp.

Featherstone Castle is now an adventure holiday centre, but it is possible to walk close enough to admire this mansion created around an old pele tower.

Featherstone Castle

The 14th. century tower, described by C.J. Bates as 'perhaps the loveliest in the county', is the nucleus of a castle which also contains the ruins of a 13th. century hall. Most of the mansion dates from Jacobean times with substantial Victorian restoration work.

The popular ghost story associated with the castle is unusual. It seems that a former Baron of Featherstonehaugh arranged the marriage of his daughter, Abigail, to a distant relative, a man called Timothy Featherstonehaugh.

Abigail resisted the wedding for as long as possible hoping that her father would relent and allow her to marry young Ridley Hardriding to whom she had given her heart. Unfortunately Ridley was a member of a family who had a longstanding feud with the baron so the old man would not consider this alternative match.

In time Abigail was forced to walk down the chapel aisle with Timothy. After the ceremony, she and her husband set off to the woods with a hunting party, promising to return for the wedding banquet.

The hunters were ambushed by Ridley Hardriding and his friends. In the bloody fight that followed everyone was slain apart from Ridley and Abigail. In true tragic style she died in his arms some minutes later from wounds received when she placed herself between her husband and lover in the midst of the battle.

When Ridley saw the consequences of his action, he was overcome with grief and stabbed himself to death. His blood was said to have drained into a hollow stone, and the ravens came down from the trees and drank it with relish.
This relic, predictably called the Raven's Stone, can still be found in the wood near the castle.

The baron and his wife were meanwhile anxiously awaiting the return of the newlyweds. At the stroke of midnight the hunting party entered the banquet hall and glided silently to their appointed seats.

The ghastly wounds, blood-drenched clothes and ashen faces, caused the baron to jump up from his seat and to cross himself. There was a sudden rushing wind and the ghostly wedding party was swept away instantly by the icy blast.

It is said that the anniversary of this terrible event is still 'celebrated' by a brief appearance of the bridal party who enter the castle gate, and sweep silently towards the ruined hall before vanishing in a 'chill mist'.

The time of this annual event can be fixed precisely at midnight. Only the date is impossible to determine, although it is said to be 'towards the longer days of the year'. Summer visitors therefore must have the best chance of beholding the most spectacular multi-haunting in Northumbria.

Exploring the Wall

Houseteads, Vindolanda and Corbridge are the most popular sites for visitors to Hadrian's Wall. The ghost hunter though is perhaps better employed elsewhere.

Cawfields is just two miles north of Haltwhistle on the north side of the B6318. Here the visitor will find the beginning of the most dramatic (three mile) section of the wall, which rises gradually eastwards towards Winshields Crag.

This popular part of the Pennine Way contains well-preserved sections of wall and one of the most complete mile castles (number 42) now in the care of the Department of the Environment.

Walking alongside the wall in this area it is easy to imagine the loneliness of soldiers patrolling between mile castles, meeting one another at a mid-way point, then turning to march back to the place where they had started.

The 12,000 or so auxiliaries who made up most of this 'security force' were recruits from all over the Roman Empire, including Britain. It is a remarkable thing that during the three centuries the wall was garrisoned there were no significant incursions by the tribes from the north.

Of course there were individuals who preferred to take a chance on scaling the wall unseen, rather than presenting themselves at recognised checkpoints. There has been no barrier created by man that it has not been profitable for someone to find a way around.

Hadrian's Wall

The story is that a young soldier, Lucius, fell in love with a local girl, Eanfritha. He defied regulations by arranging brief furtive liaisons with her as he patrolled above Milecastle 42. Eanfritha, it seems, had less regard for poor Lucius, and indeed was deliberately exploiting her charms to ensure that his attention was diverted whilst her brother, Ethelric, slipped quietly over the wall.

Ethelric became carelessly loud-mouthed about the successful 'export business' he had developed and was arrested. At first he denied the charge, but when he realised that the position was hopeless he decided to implicate Lucius in his schemes.

The soldier, when faced with the prospect of dismissal and disgrace, and the heartbreak of the cruel trick played on him, decided to take his own life. In true Roman fashion he elected to fall on his own sword, which he performed clumsily.

When Eanfritha heard what had happened she was filled with remorse, and rushed to the young soldier's side. Lucius was still alive and she stayed with him as he tenaciously hung onto life.

For a while it seemed that he may recover, but he caught a fever and died some weeks later. It is said that Eanfritha and Lucius were married a few hours before he died.

It is the ghost of this unfortunate young man that patrols the wall above Milecastle 42 to this very day. Some say he walks to atone for his negligence, and others that he still waits to meet the woman to whom he foolishly gave his heart.

This phantom soldier presents an eerie and strange vision. It is reported that he walks at the original wall level and so appears to be floating on a cushion of air. He is also one of the rare breed of ghosts whose appearances take place most frequently during daylight hours.

The Legend of the Lough

The visitor may wish to pause briefly again at Sewingshields. The mile walk from the military way to the crag (and wall) is not particularly rewarding, and the unromantically named turret 34A is perhaps of most interest to dedicated Roman historians.

However the view from the crag westwards towards Housesteads and Broomlee Lough is excellent.

There is a story that centuries ago the wealthy owner of the castle that once stood on the crag was forced to leave without taking his riches with him. He hid his treasure in a box and rowed out into Broomlee Lough and cast the box into the deep at a place that was 'unruffled by the wind'.

To make extra sure that the treasure would never be recovered he cast a special spell : it could only be recovered by twin oxen, twin horses, twin youths and a chain forged by a seventh generation blacksmith.

Some time later somebody decided it was worth trying to find the treasure and equipped himself with the necessary twins and chain. Finding a place in the lake that was 'unruffled by the wind' he lowered the chain and looped it around the treasure box. The two youths attached the ends of the chain to the oxen and horses and began to drag it towards the shore. Part of the way back the chain snapped, and the box was lost forever.

It was later revealed that the chain had not truly been forged by a seventh generation blacksmith. The grandmother of the chain maker had once slept with a handsome wandering beggar whilst her husband, the blacksmith, was away. The child of this union was adopted as part of the family, and he in time became a blacksmith, and the father of the man who made the chain.

This story seems more interesting and remarkable than claims that Broomlee Lough was the lake into which the sword Excalibur was thrown as King Arthur lay dying. There are far too many lakes with better claims. Only Broomlee Lough can claim to be associated with treasure, twins, magic chains, and seven generations of blacksmiths...

No.2 - Battle and Cattle

This motoring tour takes about six hours

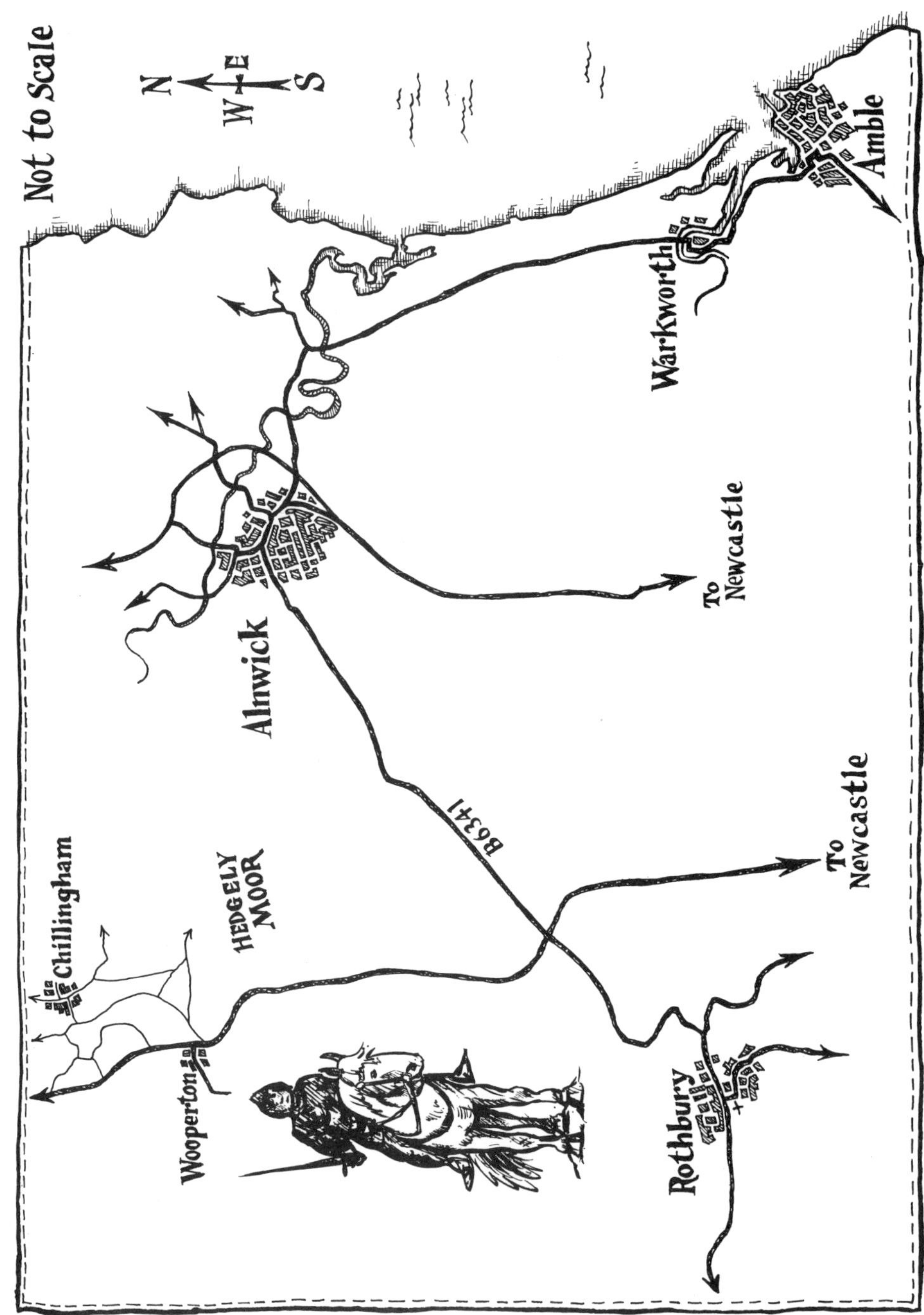
Not to Scale
N
E
W
S
Amble
Warkworth
Alnwick
To Newcastle
B6341
To Newcastle
Chillingham
HEDGELY MOOR
Wooperton
Rothbury

Northumbria - Her Infinite Variety

This tour reaches from the Northumberland coast towards the wilds of the the Cheviot Hills and the Scottish border. It captures a splendid variety of scenery that is typical of the borders.

Warkworth, close to the small fishing part of Amble, provides many visitors with their favourite memory of Northumbria. It is recommended that you park in front of the castle, and, after enjoying a visit, walk down the bank and follow the riverside path as far as the Hermitage.

The castle was carefully sited on the last bend of the River Coquet. The original motte-and-bailey construction dates from the early 11th. century, with the gatehouse and Carrickfergus Tower added in the 12th., and the keep in the 15th.

Warkworth Castle is associated primarily with the Percy family who made it their home and maintained a second fortress at Alnwick. By the middle of the 17th. century the family preference had been reversed, and Warkworth was allowed to fall into ruin.

The History of Harry Hotspur

Perhaps the best known members of the family are the third lord of Warkworth and his son, the redoubtable Harry Hotspur.

The third lord led an army in France before 1360 and was created Earl of Northumberland, and Knight of the Garter, at the coronation of Richard II in 1377.

Harry Hotspur is famous as the dashing hero of the Battles of Otterburn and Homildon Hill which did much to put Henry IV on the throne in 1399. Scenes in Shakepeare's Henry IV (Part One) remind us of the conspiracy created at Warkworth to depose the same King Henry. The dashing Harry Hotspur was soon dead - killed at the Battle of Shrewsbury in 1403. His father, the Earl, escaped to Scotland, but died at Bramham Moor in 1408.

For some years the castle and lands were forfeit, but they were later returned by Henry V when the Earl's grandson (Hotspur's son) did homage to the king in 1416.

The Mood of a Bygone Age

There can be no castle in England that captures the feeling of bygone centuries better than Warkworth. The well-preserved keep in particular provides an atmospheric warren of dark rooms in which little imagination is needed to sense the ghosts of forty generations.

At the entrance to the keep is a pit, a bottle-shaped oubliette concealed beneath wooden boards. Here the only contact with the outside world that a prisoner enjoyed was the tramping of feet overhead.

Warkworth Castle

Tom Skerratt's Curse

One such prisoner was a soldier named Tom Skeratt (or Sheratt) who was held responsible for the murder of the fourth earl in 1489. It seems likely that Tom was a minor player in an anti-Percy plot. He was arrested 'taking a fish' near to the scene of the crime at Cocklodge in Yorkshire.

Tom was consigned to the oubliette at Warkworth to await the pleasure of the fifth earl who had his principle residence two hundred miles away in the south.

It was almost two years before Tom could give an account of himself to the earl. Imprisonment had dulled his faculties to such an extent that he could no longer remember his own name. The earl took pity on him, and Tom was put in the charge of the master of hounds to be fed 'better than they (the dogs) but not again too greatly'. The poor man spent the rest of his days believing he was a member of the pack and 'howling for his meat' with the others.

This dog's life must have been healthy enough for Tom ; he outlived the fifth earl by several months. However the old earl's instruction that Tom should be interred in 'the common pit' may have been carried out because his ghost was said to torment the sixth earl (another Henry) who succeeded his father in 1527.

This seems improbable, but Henry - called 'the unthrifty ' - believed that he had been cursed with childlessness because of his father's ill-doings. The castle and estates passed to the king (Henry VIII) when he died in 1537 and were not restored to the Percy family until twenty years later.

Thomas Percy (nephew of the sixth earl) was also said to suffer the 'Skeratt curse'. His joined the unsuccessful rising of 1569, and like the third earl was soon forced to seek refuge in Scotland. He was sold by the Scots to Queen Elizabeth and beheaded at York in 1572.

His brother Henry (the eighth earl) was not allowed to receive the estates until two years later, and was not summoned to parliament until 1580. If there was such a thing as the 'Skeratt Curse' perhaps it continued, because although this earl was succeeded by his son, he died in 1584 as a prisoner in the Tower of London where he waited to answer a charge of high treason.

Twenty one years later the ninth earl also found himself a prisoner in the Tower on a charge of complicity in Catesby's Gunpowder Plot.

It was from this time that the castle fell into ruin. The tenth earl was prevented from succeeding to his title until 1632, and the eleventh earl, Joscelin, was forced to lease the castle and park to a Newcastle merchant. In 1672, Joscelin's widow allowed the estate auditor to take away 272 wagon loads of lead, timber, and other materials to build a manor house at Chirton.

It would be far-fetched to to link the decline of Warkworth over a century and a half purely to a ' curse' on the Percy family. In many ways succeeding generations of Percys can be regarded as political gamblers who successfully revived the family fortunes only to lose everything again by playing the card of rebellion. It should also be remembered that by the time Warkworth Castle was being carted away in wagon loads it had long ceased to be a family residence.

Tom Skeratt's 'curse' may be seen perhaps as symptomatic of the troubled history of the Percy family, rather than as having any particular historical significance.

A Grey Lady?

The only other supernatural phenomena linked with Warkworth Castle are rather unsatisfactory reports of a 'grey lady' who is seen occasionally wandering around the keep.

The wooded riverside walk below the castle walls is one of the most enjoyable in Northumbria. As the visitor follows the course of the Coquet it is tempting to look back to catch a glimpse of the keep reflected in the water.

This area, known locally as the 'butts', provides some of the best salmon fishing in the region. About a mile upstream is a jetty from which there are seasonal 'boat trips' over the water to the hermitage.

The unusual building, now hidden by trees, contains a chapel, a sacristy and a tiny solar carved out of the limestone.

The Legend of Sir Bertram and the Fair Isabel

The most popular version of the story of 'The Warkworth Hermit' begins with the inscription over the hermitage doorway which in translation reads : 'My tears have been my meat night and day'.

The unfortunate man shedding these tears is said to be a knight called Sir Bertram of Bothal. He promised the beautiful Isabel, daughter of Lord Widdrington, that he would perform some daring deed to prove himself worthy of marrying her.

The opportunity for heroism arose in a border skirmish in which Bertram excelled himself in arms before a Scottish sword smashed the helmet from his head. He was taken to Wark Castle to recover from his wounds. A message was sent to Isabel who set out immediately to be with her betrothed in his hour of need.

Isabel was ambushed on her journey and taken to a Scottish chieftain's castle. As soon as Bertram recovered he rode to Isabel's home. He was told of course that she had travelled to join him at Wark. Realising immediately that Isabel had been captured, he swore that he would not rest until he had found her.

Bertram and his brother set out separately to make enquiries about the whereabouts of the lady. Eventually Bertram learned from a monk that a 'princess' was being held at a particular fortress. The owner of this fortress was a Scottish chieftain who had previously tried to court Isabel, and Bertram had no doubt that this was the place.

He arrived at the fortress weary from his journey and hid in a nearby cave. He watched the fortress continuously, until on the evening of the third day he caught a glimpse of his beloved at the window of a high tower. Exhausted by his vigil he fell at last into a deep sleep.

When he awoke, he looked out if the cave entrance and saw a figure in Scottish clansman's dress carrying a lady down a rope ladder from the tower. He rushed to the spot and intercepted the 'clansman' as he invited Isabel to climb onto a waiting horse. A hefty blow from Bertram's sword brought the man to the ground, and despite Isabel's shouts he was not inclined to mercy. He raised his sword again and the second blow was fatal to the 'clansman', and to poor Isabel who tried to push between the two men.

Moments later Bertram realised with horror that he had killed both Isabel and his own brother. His self-imposed penance was to build the lonely hermitage on the Coquet and to live there in solitude and silence for the rest of his days.

It is said that Bertram did not speak again until the last moment of his life. The boy who brought him food from the castle each day found him hunched up before a meagre fire one winter's morning. Bertram was now very frail and almost freezing to death. The boy told him that he would bring some logs.

Bertram slumped forwards and seemed to murmur something. The boy moved towards Bertram anticipating some instruction.

He was close enough to hear the one word - ' Isabel ' - spoken with the knight's dying breath.

A century or more ago the ghost of Sir Bertram of Bothal was regularly reported to maintain a silent vigil at the hermitage. Some sightings were of a young man in full battle armour, and others (more likely perhaps) were of a weary old man in the simple brown cloak of a hermit. The only consistency in all these reports is that the spectre was like the grave itself - utterly silent.

A more modern ghost story is linked to the hermitage. It is not supported by much evidence, but it is frequently retold in local schools. It has an unusual theme and it is interesting to speculate on its origins.

The following version is typical of the way the story is told. It is in the form of a short story obviously written for children, but it is well worth retelling.

The Hermit of Warkworth

Elizabeth had heard her little sister scream many times before. Sometimes she would scream in anger, and sometimes with pleasure. What she heard, as she set up the things on the grass, was neither of this sounds. It was a scream of terror.

Elizabeth jumped to her feet and looked towards the river. What she saw there made her lips tremble and the colour drained from her cheeks.

Amanda had fallen into the water. Elizabeth could see only her black hair and a small hand raised above her head. Already she was being pulled downstream by the fast-flowing current. Soon all she could make out were white flecks of foam where the river crashed against the rocks. She began to run wildly downstream, but suddenly she heard a sound that made her stop. It was the sound of splashing.

Round the bend of the river came a small boat. Oars were dipping in and out of the water. At the front of the boat was a large man rowing. At the back there was a small dark-haired girl.

As the boat came close Elizabeth thought they made a strange picture. He was taller than any man she had ever seen. He wore the long brown habit of a monk and had the most striking pale blue eyes. As he lifted Amanda from the boat she looked like a toy doll in his enormous arms. Though he was soaking wet, she knew that this must be the ferryman who rowed visitors across the river. He told her his name was Brother Michael and that he lived at the hermitage.

A few days later Elizabeth returned to the riverside. She carried with her the largest duffle coat that she could find in any of the shops. It was a present for Brother Michael.

She walked to the place where the little boat was moored. She had hoped to see Brother Michael, but found a silver haired old man sitting in the boat.

She explained to the ferryman that she had a present to take to the hermitage. He looked at her closely and told her he was surprised. After all, nobody lived there any more. What was more, on the previous Monday - when Amanda had fallen into the water - sickness had kept him away from work. The little boat would have been tied up all day by the waterside.

Elizabeth wondered why Brother Michael had left so soon. Something was not quite right. She gave the ferryman his fee and asked to be rowed across.

As he was rowing the old man recalled that there had been a young Brother Michael who lived for a while at the hermitage. He was a famous swimmer - and a brave man too. Many times he had jumped into the water to save a life without any thought for his own safety.

At last Elizabeth understood. The kindly Brother Michael had returned. He had heard Amanda's screams and knew what they meant. He must have been close to the ferryman's boat and had borrowed it to help with the rescue. When he got close enough he plunged into the water, lifted Amanda safely into the boat, and rowed upstream.

Elizabeth began to realise how fortunate her sister had been. She remembered how helpless she had felt. If Brother Michael had not returned, it was certain that Amanda would have perished in the rushing flow of the river.

She told the ferryman what had happened. He shook his head slowly. He told her that Brother Michael had injured himself on the rocks when he rescued someone else from the river. He was a strong man but had only just managed to swim ashore.

But Elizabeth insisted that she had met Brother Michael.

Again the ferryman shook his head. Then he told Elizabeth more of the history. The brave monk, he recalled, had died from his injuries, and that had happened more than a 100 years ago...

Around and About in Alnwick

The market town of Alnwick deserves more than a cursory visit. Here is a brief outline of the possibilities.

Fragments of the old town walls (begun in 1433) show that Alnwick, in common with other prosperous border towns, soon learnt the importance of adequate fortifications.

The eighty foot high Tenantry Column was built in 1815 through the subscription of a thousand tenants to thank the Duke of Northumberland for reducing their rents. This was no mark of respect. The Duke had increased rents threefold in previous years and the tenants wished to demonstrate their solidarity, and their distrust of the Duke's rare gesture of 'philanthropy'. The Tenantry Column is also known as the 'Farmers' Folly'.

The archway through which the visitor will enter the town is called the Hotspur Tower. It is the only one of the original (four) medieval gateways to survive. The town centre contains a fine Market Cross, a

Hotspur Tower, Bondgate, Alnwick

Shambles, an unusual fountain (St. Michael's Pant), an 18th. century Town Hall, and the distinctive Northumberland Hall which dates from 1826.

The continuation of the main street - Bondgate - leads to Narrowgate and the Old Cross Inn. This 18th. century hostelry is better known locally as 'The Dirty Bottles'. These are still displayed in a small window facing the street.

In early Victorian times an innkeeper died whilst dressing the window. Local superstition has not encouraged anyone to risk completing the task...

St. Michael's Church dates from Norman times, but the 'modern building' is mainly 15th. century in origin. The church contains a rare 14th. century Flemish chest and an unusual stair turret which was used as a lookout post. In times of danger someone could be placed in the small viewing chamber to watch for a beacon signal from Hefferlaw Tower two miles away. Alnwick is a popular centre for Scottish tourists, but the warlike visitors who marched into the town from the north in former times were not considering a cup of coffee and a jam doughnut in one of the excellent tearooms.

The Windsor of the North

Alnwick Castle main entrance

The impressive Alnwick Castle is still the home of the Duke of Northumberland and consequently visitors are only invited to see parts of it. Nevertheless a visit is highly recommended.

The castle, sometimes called 'The Windsor of the North', contains art treasures and fine furnishings and china. Visitors may also see lavishly decorated apartments, the Keep, Armoury, Dungeon, Library, Guard Chamber, and the Museum of British and Roman Antiquities.

Alnwick, like Bamburgh, is frequently used by film-makers as an impressive backdrop to their recreations of the medieval world, and locals will proudly list the number of productions in which they have worked as 'extras'.

It is probably the cinema that gives the visitor the sense of 'deja vue ' when he sees the castle. The most impressive and obviously cinematic view of the castle is from the Lion Bridge over the river Aln below the town. Robin Hood, Ivanhoe and Richard the Lion Heart have all successfully attacked the castle from the green pastures near the bridge in recent years.

Although there are claims for Saxon origins, by Northumbrian standards the castle may not be particularly old. Begun by a Norman knight (Ivo de Vesci) in 1135, it came to prominence as a Percy stronghold in the 14th. century, from which time most of the construction dates. By the middle of the 15th. century the external appearance of the buildings was very much as it is today. It is considered by some to be the most impressive medieval fortress in Britain.

The history of this castle is again linked to the fortunes of the Percy family.

In the 16th century the favoured Percy stronghold was still Warkworth, so Alnwick began to fall into ruin. A century later, when the preference was reversed, the new Duke of Northumberland (the first of the present line) began the restoration of the castle. This process was completed in early Victorian times.

Magnificent though Alnwick is as a fortress, it is a disappointment to the ghost hunter.

The Chorus of Wails

However, there are claims that when the wind is in the right direction on fine autumn evenings a 'chorus of wailing' can be clearly heard on the pastures below the castle. That the sound comes from the castle is not disputed, but what it represents is less certain. Perhaps the most satisfactory theory relates to a tragic episode after the Battle of Dunbar in September 1650.

After 'taming the Scots' some six thousand prisoners were brought by Cromwell's army to Alnwick and locked up within the castle bailey. A week later half of them were dead from starvation, and most of the rest died on the forced march from Alnwick to Durham.

Some say that the 'chorus of wailing' are the voices of the defeated soldiers, realising that it is their fate to die without seeing their homes and families again. Others say that the sound is that of their womenfolk who walked the long weary miles from Dunbar to petition the captain of the garrison.

The second version is perhaps more attractive, but there is no historical evidence for the 'women's march'. Indeed it is an improbable event - most of the soldiers' families would have been scattered around Scotland and the borders, and those who were 'camp followers' would hardly have risked following the prisoners to the Cromwellian stronghold of Alnwick.

This is a ghost story that is as insubstantial in fact as a party political broadcast.

The delightful rural journey between Alnwick and Powburn is one of the few in Northumbria where it is possible to get lost. This is because of poor signposting and a myriad of small country road and farm tracks. The ghost hunter is therefore given the appropriate health warning...

Percy's Leap

About two miles north of Powburn on the A 679 there is a layby opposite a sawmill. Here a clump of trees marks an unusual historical site.

In April 1464 a Lancastrian army under the leadership of Sir Ralph Percy ambushed Edward IV's soldiers here at the Battle of Hedgeley Moor. Sir Ralph's intention was to attack the king's general, Lord Montague, before his soldiers could link up with a larger Scottish army.

Sir Ralph charged the Yorkist line in true Percy style, But his horse was wounded as he leapt over two large boulders. Some minutes later Sir Ralph himself was mortally injured.

As he died he is reputed to have said cryptically : 'I have saved the bird in my bosom'.

This may possibly mean that he died for the 'rightful' monarch, Henry VI, or perhaps he had kept the secret of where Henry and his wife (Margaret of Anjou) were hiding. Such were the political tides of the Wars of the Roses it is impossible to fully accept either of these meanings. Anyway, it was not long before the Percy family changed sides again...

Two stones on the ground are said to mark 'Percy's Leap'. There is a distance of about seven metres between them.

Perhaps the visitor may expect a leaping phantom ghost on horseback at this spot but nothing about the Percy family is any more predictable than their political loyalties.

The Black Horse

The phantom of Hedgeley Moor is not the man, but the horse. It is said that a coal black riderless animal is seen from time to time galloping over the moor in the direction of what would have been the Yorkist army's line on that spring day in 1464.

It is a ghostly gallop with neither the sound or mark of a hoof on the ground...

Midway between Alnwick and Wooler is the hamlet of Wooperton. The lovely old Hall is private property but it can been seen to advantage from close to the 'village' goose pond.

There is an interesting story associated with the hall.

The Legend of Black Adam

Black Adam, a notorious thief, had word of a 'society' wedding here. He burst in upon the assembled guests and grabbed hold of the bride. With a knife at her throat he demanded that the guests hand over all their valuables which he placed in the cavernous pockets of his long black cloak.

As he began to make his escape down the long flight of stairs towards his horse waiting near the pond, the bride began to scream. He silenced her with a slash from his blade, leaped into his saddle and galloped away.

The groom ran to to his bride's side, but she had already breathed her last. In silent rage the young man leapt upon the tethered mount of one of his guests, and rode 'like the devil himself' after Black Adam.

Gradually he broke down the distance between them and Black Adam was no more than 'the length of horse' ahead as they came towards the Henhole Gorge.

The men leapt the gorge together. Perhaps their horses crashed together in the air because both men plunged to their deaths on the rocks below.

The Ghostly Groom

The ghost of the young bridegroom has been reported dashing down the steps in the darkness from Wooperton Hall, pausing briefly at the place where his murdered bride lay, leaping to the saddle of a phantom steed, and vanishing as the ringing sound of hooves fade slowly into the distance.

The Ghosthunter's Tale

Simon Griffith, an amateur ghosthunter from Northampton, describes his own encounter with the ghostly groom.

" *Mark (my cousin) and I had given up all hope of seeing anything. It was a disappointment because Wooperton had seemed promising. We'd waited in the car for hours until the moon was set, then Mark had dozed off. I could feel the heaviness of my own eyes and decided that a walk might help to keep me awake*"

" *I took a quick look at the hall, but there was nothing unusual going on. It was as silent as the grave. It had been a clear cool night but as I wandered off down the road things began to change. The fog came down like an icy blanket and what little breeze there was evaporated.*"

" *I felt warm so and pulled off my jacket and slung it over my arm. It was then that I first had the feeling of not being alone. There were shapes moving around in the mist and the indistinct murmurings of human voices. I knew better than to give myself away so I just stood where I was and waited. There was a thrill of anticipation, but I was frightened too. Something was going to happen for sure.*"

" *The voices became clearer. The female ones were easier to pick out. I heard 'wedding party', 'bride' and words that sounded like 'pretty Lady Alice.*"

" The shapes floated around me. Even if I could have seen more clearly I doubt that they were substantial. These were not ghosts, but wraith like creatures - almost part of the mist itself. I think they represented a kind of 'snapshot in time' that was now locked into the ether. I knew that they were harmless, but their very presence meant that something very unpleasant had happened here. These wraiths or airy spirits were the bit-part players, the observers of a most dreadful event. "

" The voices became shrill and then turned into a cacophony of wild screams. The sound washed around me. It was like the chattering of monkeys in the rainforest at sunset. I could feel my breath coming more rapidly and the hairs on my neck were standing out. I cursed Mark for falling asleep in the car. I badly needed his company now. "

" Then I heard the ringing sound of horseshoes on the ground. The first galloping rider was past me almost before I realised it. I edged towards the road to get a good view of the one that I knew would follow. At first I thought I'd be disappointed. Any ghosthunter will tell you that seconds count like minutes when you're antiicipating a manifestation."

" The mist obscured him until he was almost upon me. A clear patch of moonlight broke through at the same moment. The ghost was crouched low in the saddle of the phantom steed. The light captured a pale young face - more of a boy than man. He kicked with his spurs as he passed me and the horse chomped at the bit in his mouth. "

" Then he was gone and the echoes of hoof beats were soon muffled by the fog. At first I was exhilarated and light headed, but the mood changed quickly to one of dark depression. I walked slowly back to the car. "

Entangled Legends?

There has been speculation that the fate of Black Adam and that of Sir Ralph Percy - who both died after coming to grief after famous horseback leaps - are somehow entangled legends. It is most unlikely to be so since the fate of Sir Ralph at least is well documented, and there are several centuries and a great mass of the Cheviot Hills to separate the events.

There is certainly no confusion about which castle has the most outstanding claim to be the most haunted in Northumbria. It has been especially saved for the final leg of the tour.

A Brief History of Chillingham

The ornately carved tombs in Chillingham Church

Before exploring Chillingham Castle a brief visit to the church is recommended. This delightful and beautifully sited building has retained much of its 12th. century structure and the magnificently carved table tomb of Sir Ralph Grey and his wife Elizabeth, the first owners of the nearby castle.

The castle, unlike many others in Northumbria, was not fortified until the middle of the 14th. century. It was to be attacked many times in the centuries that followed, and was dismantled after the Battle of Flodden in 1513.

In the 17th. century the famous architect Inigo Jones was engaged to re-design the castle to give better accommodation and greater comfort. The building we see today is still very much the Inigo Jones model, looking perhaps more like a chateau than a castle it is nevertheless a most imposing building.

During the last century the castle fell into a state of great decay. The present owner, Sir Humphrey Wakefield, has recently set about the task of restoring the castle and gardens to their former glory. His progress already has been remarkable, and hauntings apart, Chillingham Castle is a fascinating place to visit, with the stomach-churning torture chamber perhaps the most obvious attraction!

For the ghost hunter, Chillingham is the most appropriately named place in Northumberland.

Leonora Tankerville's singular (1925) account of a macabre discovery in her bedroom is the best place to begin an account of the castle's supernatural specialities.

Two Macabre Discoveries

She wrote : 'In my own bedroom, a few years ago, some stones fell accidentally from the wall, and there, in its thickness, stood two grinning skeletons where the fireplace now is, bones of a man and a child, close by the trap door that opens to the stone arches of the vaults below.'

'Who were these prisoners, I wonder! Were they some awkward neighbour and his heir? Some enemy caught in a border raid, and of whose remains was it unsafe to let any trace be found? Were they walled in alive or dead? I know not. Only this I know, that room today is full of peace and calm.'

Leonora Tankerville mentions a second discovery of bones at Chillingham.

When a lower walled-up dungeon was opened workmen found the 'wonderfully preserved' seated figure of a man that dissolved quickly as air rushed into the chamber.

The Radiant Boy

One of the best known apparitions was the 'Radiant Boy'. According to the story when midnight sounded the cries and moans of a child could be heard in the Pink room. The noises always came from a place close to a passage cut through a ten foot thick wall. As the cries faded away 'a bright halo of light' formed, and this light surrounded the figure of a young boy dressed in blue.

Fragments of blue cloth and the bones 'of a boy of tender years' were later discovered in the wall. The remains were buried in consecrated ground and the apparition was never seen again.

The Ghost of Lady Mary

One phantom still very much on the active list is that of Lady Mary Berkely.

This unfortunate lady was the wife of a 17th. century Earl Tankerville who 'ran away' with her sister, Lady Henrietta, creating a famous scandal of the day.

Lady Mary was left at Chillingham in 'her dark and lonely castle with only a fatherless baby girl as her companion'.

The rustle of her dress is still said to be heard along the corridors and stairs and her progress is accompanied by a chilling blast of air.

A Gathering of Ghosts

The list of ghosts at Chillingham is impressive. According to Leonora Tankerville again there is a Dominican Abbess who gazes longingly towards the hills of Scotland as she walks on the parapet of a tower, a young officer whose spectre returned briefly to the castle at the hour of his death, and the restless spirit of a chef who committed suicide.

Other ghosts associated with Chillingham include the following interesting pair.

The first is a medieval soldier who bravely staggers to the main entrance with the heavy burden of half a quiver full of arrows in his back. It is said that he brings a timely warning of an impending Scottish attack on the castle. This is a spectre that has been unemployed in recent years.

The second is an unidentified headless gentleman who is seen from time to time wandering around the Italian gardens at the west side of the house. It is understood that this is the site of the former jousting ground so perhaps the gentleman concerned came second in a contest with a rival?

Finally there are ghostly noises associated with the castle's oubliette which is much the same type as that found at Alnwick and Warkworth.

The dungeon was constructed below the north-east corner of the castle.

In its floor there is a trapdoor leading to the even deeper oubliette. This was a place where former barons of Chillingham could imprison their enemies (and occasionally unwelcome guests) and literally forget them.

There is little sound from this deepest dungeon except when the trapdoor is opened. But it is said that weird echos, and a strange combination of wails and groans can be heard from time to time around that corner of the building. It would be impossible to leave Chillingham without mentioning one of Northumbria's most popular tourist attractions and the legend associated with it.

The famous white cattle have grazed in the three hundred acre park around the castle since the 13th. century. They are Britain's last surviving wild herd and direct descendants of the wild cattle that roamed all over Europe and Britain before the Roman invasion.

Centuries of inbreeding have decreased their size but they remain a major curiosity. It is said they have the same colouring as fairy cattle and that they will kill anyone who touches them.

In 1872 the King of the Herd had the 'distinction of being shot' by the future King of England (Edward V11). This single incident created such strong Northumbrian ill-feeling against the Prince of Wales that he was 'most heavily protected' on his subsequent visits to the region.

It has been said that if local people had been able to lay hands on the Prince after the shooting he would not have lived to inherit his mother's throne.

Who is to say there is no truth in an old legend?

Opening Times :

Warkworth Castle : Open daily during season. October - March, Sunday afternoons only.

Alnwick Castle : Open May - September. Closed Fridays.

Chillingham Castle : Open May - September. Closed Tuesdays.

Chillingham Castle

No.3 - Ghosts of the Coast

This linear motoring tour takes about three hours

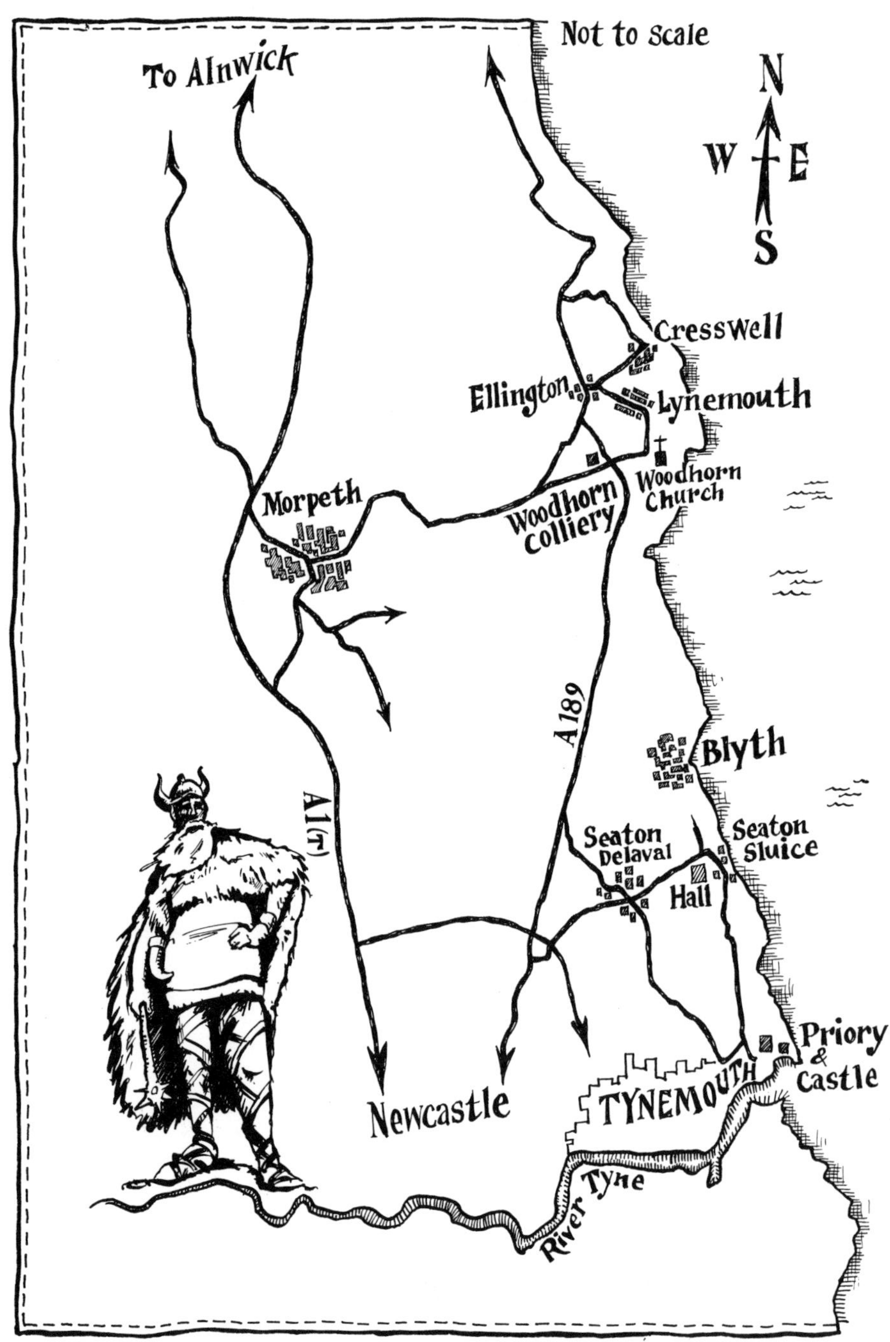
Not to Scale
N
W
E
S
To Alnwick
Cresswell
Ellington
Lynemouth
Woodhorn Church
Woodhorn Colliery
Morpeth
A189
Blyth
A1(T)
Seaton Delaval
Hall
Seaton Sluice
Priory & Castle
Newcastle
TYNEMOUTH
River Tyne

A Changing Landscape

The coastline that stretches north from the mouth of the Tyne is an area neglected by visitors. This has probably much to do with the popular impression of traditional industries creating a landscape of factory chimneys and pitheads.

This is outdated, unfair and inaccurate.

It is true to say that compared to rural Northumberland this area is a hive of activity. But the comparison is relative. You can walk on hillsides and beaches elsewhere and not meet another human for hours. Here clusters of small towns and villages flow into one another without obvious boundaries or demarcation. Between the clusters are large pockets of agricultural land. The conurbation that runs through North Shields, Tynemouth, Cullercoats and Whitley Bay is densely populated. To the north only Blyth and Ashington (with a combined population of around 60,000) are places of any significance.

It is an area that has changed immensely in recent years. Whitley Bay may still be the Blackpool of the North-East, but it is also leafy Arcadia Avenue. Ashington, once the largest mining village in Europe, is fast becoming a bustling little market town.

It is an area of stark contrasts and full of possibilities for the ardent ghost hunter.

The Oldest Church in Northumbria

Tynemouth is dominated by the impressive castle and priory. The first monastery was established here in the seventh century, and there are claims that this was the site of the oldest church in Northumbria. It is also the burial place of two saints - Oswin (who was murdered in 651) and Henry of Coquet who expired in mysterious circumstances in 1127.

Intermittent Viking raids encouraged the monks to develop and improve their defences, and the Danes were routed and driven off in 832. Thirty-three years later they returned and razed both the monastery and church to the ground. Contemporary accounts describe this attack as a terrible massacre. Even nuns of St.Hilda, who had come here for safety, were brutally murdered.

Earl Tostig made Tynemouth his fortress during the reign of Edward the Confessor, and had intentions of refounding the monastery. Provoked by banishment, he took up arms against King Harold and was killed at the Battle of Stamford Bridge in 1066.

The monastery was revived briefly by the Benedictines of Durham at the end of the eleventh century, and finally successfully by the St.Albans Chapter at the beginning of the twelfth. The monastery was dissolved in 1539, and the only significant remains are those of the church which was in regular use until 1688.

Tynemouth Priory

The castle continued to have a military function into modern times though a serious fire in the gatehouse rendered that building unsafe in 1936. Gun emplacements (covering the mouth of the Tyne) were maintained throughout the Second World War.

This strange alliance of the church and the military throughout the centuries explains why Tynemouth's most celebrated ghost, Prior Olaf, walks the walls looking for Viking raiders.

The Legend of Prior Olaf

The legend has it that Olaf himself was a Dane well versed in the arts of rape, pillage and the sword. After a disastrous raid he was wounded and left for dead on a beach near Seaton Sluice. Monks nursed him back to health, he took Holy vows, and in the fulness of time became leader of the order.

Clearly he feared the possibility of a Viking raid at Tynemouth and could often be seen gazing out to sea from the central parapet of the gate tower. On the day that the dreaded red-brown sails were sighted he was found praying at the shrine of St.Oswin for deliverance from the threat of the Norsemen.

The defences had been well mustered and the monks refused the demands of the Viking leader, Eric, to hand over the monastery treasure. In the battle that followed they made telling use of hot oil and boiling lead, followed by a shower of heavy stones. Discouraged by such resistance the Viking horde retreated to their boats and sailed away to seek easier pickings elsewhere.

The casualties were brought to the monastery hospital and tended by the monks. One who proved to be beyond these ministrations was the same Eric who had led the raid. He had suffered the misfortune of standing directly beneath a position on the walls from which two large boulders had descended. When the monks realised that they had in their hands the body of the Viking leader himself, Olaf was summoned to the hospital.

Olaf recognised the dead man as his younger brother and he became distraught with grief and anguish. After arranging the burial of his brother he retired to the chapel and asked to be left alone for silent prayer and contemplation. For some hours the monks honoured his wish, but later became anxious about their leader's suffering and his solitary vigil.

They entered the chapel and found Olaf cold and dead on his knees before the altar.

A Ghostly Monk

It is in fine weather when the wind blows from the east that a ghostly monk is most frequently seen. Sometimes he stands silently on the parapet gazing out over the water. Sometimes he marches tirelessly round the walls with his habit billowing silently in the breeze.

It is presumed that the ghost is that of Olaf. After all, the tragic circumstances of his death do seem to merit a good haunting. The true identity of the ghostly monk though is uncertain as the face of the apparition is always hidden by a the cowl of his habit.

Representing another era, but also looking out longingly over the water, is the nearby statue of Admiral Cuthbert Collingwood. This is the gentleman who assumed command of the British fleet at Trafalgar after the death of Nelson. He was eventually buried alongside him in St. Paul's Cathedral.

Wandering Willie

It was near this statue some years ago on the banks of the Tyne that the body of a small border collie dog was found. This was the celebrated 'Wandering Willie'.

The dog became separated from his master, a shepherd, who used to cross the Tyne each day on the row-boat ferry. It is not clear why the shepherd never returned to claim him, but the dog waited loyally, except for excursions into Tynemouth in search of food, until he died several years later.

The mortal remains of the dog are preserved at The Turk's Head public house opposite to the castle, but his ghost continues to sniff around the alleyways of Tynemouth and has also been reported close to the Collingwood statue where he sits patiently waiting for his master to return.

There were once deep caves in the cliffs on the north side of the castle. Those who take the steep steps down onto the sandy cove can clearly see the erosion that has damaged the rocky spur of land which is the subject of so much legend.

The Pirate Treasure

A deep cave was once reputed to hold pirate treasure which was protected by dragons. Quite how the pirates intended to recover their property is not clear - possibly with the help of a magic spell incanted by the wizard who conveniently lived in an adjacent cave. If this could be proved to do so, it would be one of the earliest historical examples of the employment of a middleman to facilitate hazardous financial transactions.

The Legend of Walter the Bold

A more elaborate story about the caves bears an uncanny resemblance to a type of popular computer game.

One of the larger caves was called 'Jingling Geordie's Hole'. It used to contain two chambers, from one of which there was a passageway that lead to two vaults. In these vaults there was a huge quantity of treasure guarded by evil dwarfs with specially trained demons and dragons.

A knight, appropriately named Walter the Bold, set out to Tynemouth to acquire the treasure for himself. He climbed the rocks towards the caves and entered a narrow tunnel which lead to a labyrinth of other passages. Eventually he encountered a random selection of dwarfs, demons and dragons, who made it clear to him that he was an unwelcome visitor.

Sir Walter was forced backwards by the searing heat of the dragon's breath until he came to a yawning chasm which he leapt despite the weighty handicap of his armour.

The keepers of the labyrinth were unable to imitate this athletic prowess and Sir Walter found himself on a rocky ledge faced by an enormous door and a bugle on a golden chain. The bold knight sounded the bugle, and the door magically swung open to reveal a treasure vault.

Sir Walter used his sturdy helmet as a improvised bucket and collected selected handfuls of precious stones. Then he left the vault by another passage which in turn led to the open mouth of a large cave - presumably 'Jingling Geordie's Hole'. From there it was a simple matter of climbing down a precarious rockface with his helmet tucked under an arm before escaping on his milk-white steed which was patiently waiting on the beach below.

There are as many versions of this story as there are people who would tell it. Only the ending in every case is common - Sir Walter becomes the wealthy lord of hundreds of castles, marries a ravishingly beautiful princess, and, naturally enough, lives happily ever afterwards.

The greater part of 'Jingling Geordie's Hole', also known as the 'Jingling Man's Hole' or 'Merlin's Cave', vanished in a massive land-slip more than a hundred years ago. What remains are two unimpressive small caves. Stories abound of treasure and a network of secret passages beneath the castle and priory. Limited excavations have failed to unlock these mysteries.

The South Northumberland Coast

After passing through Cullercoats and Whitley Bay you reach the most southerly coastal part of Northumberland at Seaton Sluice. Here, you will recall, Prior Olaf stepped ashore a thousand years ago with a long sword and a hairy band of Viking warriors.

The same beach was a favoured site for witch burning, particularly in the middle ages, because the tide here could be relied on to remove all charred remains within a few hours.

The Witch Trials

The last witch trail was in 1712, but during the infamous witch-finder period of the 17th. century, trails and executions reached epidemic proportions. Torture to extract confessions was illegal by this time, but the methods of Matthew Hopkins and others - with their technique of pricking to find anaesthetic areas of the body - made a mockery of the law.

The favoured method was to strip the victim, blindfold her, then feel all over her body for some area of hard skin. The pin was then gently inserted. If the woman did not cry out, or the place start to bleed, she was instructed to find the pin herself. If her hand moved to the wrong part of her body it was accepted the devil had touched the area around the pin. This was sufficient evidence to convict her as a witch.

The famous Scottish witchfinder, Kinkaid, visited this area in the 1690's. Northumberland was beyond the sphere of his jurisdiction but he happily acted as a paid 'adviser' to the court.

There were no convictions during his visit despite vigorous prickings carefully supervised by the expert. He was an angry man when he mounted the stagecoach for Edinburgh. The English it seems were 'blind and ignorant of the ways of witchery.'

He was more successful at home in Scotland - where torture was still legally practised. He enjoyed his last success north of the border in 1722.

The Devil's Fires

The witch burnings of the middle ages were in all probability rather more like lynchings. There are only sketchy accounts of events at Seaton Sluice, but there is little doubt that the burnings were a favourite spectator sport in the 13th. and 14th. centuries.

During the Cromwellian years the persecution of witchery reached its zenith. The beach at Seaton Sluice served once again for the convenient disposal of the cadavers. Those found guilty were first ducked either in the sea or in a pond that formed part of the village sewer. They were then whipped, had their teeth torn out, and were finally released from their agonies by the hangman. The mutilated corpses were bound to a hurdle on the beach and had burning faggots heaped upon them.

Thomas Mulligan, variously described as a 'merchant traveller' or 'gentleman of the road', vividly described one such execution in 1653 :

" *There was joy upon (their) faces as the poor wretch was taken out. She was a little more than a girl of perhaps 18 summers. First the priest demanded that she recant which she would not, claiming yet to be innocent of that which had condemned her. They cut her hair crudely with shears and stripped her in the sight of all. She cursed them, yet they laughed at her outrage.*"

" *I could not bear to watch the torture, yet my ears witnessed the screams as the lash tore again and again into her flesh. Beyond that I believe she was insensible, for when (her) teeth were drawn by the surgeon there was no sound from her. I later heard that (the) jaw was cracked as he began his business. When the noose was fixed they became hushed and one or two made (the) sign of the cross.*"

" *At last she was transported to the shore for burning and the column of people followed. Faggots were brought, made gross by the stench of straw taken afresh from the byres. They cheered the flames but fell silent again as* the heat drove *them some distance away. The publican brought a cart of ale which was plentifully consumed. They ate much bread and salted fish.* "

The matter-of-factness of Mulligan's report suggests that the event was not particularly unusual. The beach at Seaton Sluice does not attract many visitors, but that may have more to do with its location than its unhappy history. Those who walk there do sometimes mention 'cold spots' that have no meteorological explanation. There has been talk too of fires - often clearly seen from some way off - that seem to disappear when investigated.

The little harbour was created by Sir Ralph Delaval in 1628 and this was improved by a cut made through the rock in the 1750's. If some parts of the southern section of the Northumberland coastline lack charm and character you will nevertheless be impressed by the rows of red-roofed cottages and the welcome refreshment available at the King's Arms overlooking the harbour.

A White Lady

Seaton Delaval Hall a mile away is a Vanburgh masterpiece commissioned by Admiral George Delaval in 1720. Neither the admiral or the architect lived to see it completed, Sir George dying tragically after a fall from a horse.

Seaton Delaval Hall

The house has been severely damaged by fire on two occasions and restoration is still far from complete. Nevertheless it is well worth a visit, as is the nearby tiny 14th. century church which contains family memorials and 13th. century effigies of a knight and his lady.

The ghost here is an unknown 'white lady' who is most commonly seen floating up and down the spiral staircase to the east of the great doorway. She is a silent spectre with a fixed smile that has been described both as 'serene' and 'chilling'.

As you drive along the uninspiring roads immediately to the north, you may take solace from the anticipation of many fine hauntings at the end of your journey.

The Supernatural Underground

The collieries of Blyth and Ashington are rich sources of supernatural phenomena. The nature of mining means that there is usually little for the visitor to see that can capture the atmosphere of toil and tragedy underground.

A visit to the Woodhorn Colliery Museum at Ashington goes some way towards putting this right. The museum is still at the development stage, and original pithead equipment is in the process of restoration. It will be a fitting record and memorial for those generations of rugged and cheerful man who understood and accepted the daily dangers of their working lives.

The silent pit head at Woodhorn

Woodhorn closed in 1979, but coal was still mined at the Ashington pit until ten years later. Miles of coalface workings underground interlinked these two great collieries with a third pit a couple of miles north at Lynemouth.

The Woodhorn pit head is a place for quiet reflection now. The noises, sights and sounds of yesterday can be conjured up only through the imagination.

Is it the imagination that causes some people to hear the sound of women weeping near this spot?

In 1916 news of disaster travelled rapidly along the long rows of Ashington's terraced houses. Wives and mothers rushed to the pithead for news of their menfolk, not knowing that some of them were already buried forever deep underground.

There have been sightings too of an old miner who sits near this spot sobbing quietly with blackened hands covering his face. Those who go to comfort him find that he is no more substance than a shadow that vanishes mysteriously into the ether.

A classic and recurring tale concerns a group of men crossing between one working gallery and another, before being sent back in the direction from which they had arrived by a young pit deputy who warned them it was unsafe to proceed.

Minutes later a gas explosion brought down the roof of the empty gallery. Naturally the men tried to seek out the pit deputy to thank him for the timely warning.

They were unable to find the man and were surprised to learn that the explosion had been entirely unforeseen. There had been no warning and no instruction given. Only a newspaper photograph pasted in a scrapbook offered any hint as to who the man may have been. The story accompanying the picture told of the tragic death of a young deputy caused by the collapse of a gallery some twenty-five years earlier.

A more recent story concerns a nightwatchman who saw two men in miner's clothes crossing a store yard. He challenged them, and when they turned away, he began to move after them. He gave up the race when they vanished into a brick wall.

It should be recorded that the nightwatchman in question had developed the habit of carrying a large hip-flask of whisky as fortification against cold winter nights, and at the time he reported the incident the flask had already been emptied. It may therefore have been the watchman, rather than the vanishing miners, who properly belonged to the world of spirits.

The King's Sister-in-Law

The ancient Woodhorn Church

It is worth a brief diversion to circle round the north of Newbiggin and take a brief look at the ancient Woodhorn Church, now a museum and cultural centre in the care of Wansbeck District Council.

The building has been altered many times, but the traditional alternations of short and long stones seen just below the base of the tower are proof of Saxon origins.

The church contains a most singular relic - the 13th. century effigy of Agnes de Valence, wife of Hugh Baliol, whose brother Edward was briefly King of Scotland.

The effigy is regarded as one of the best examples of 13th. century monumental sculpture in Britain.

A Ghostly Cyclist

The ghostly cyclist who haunts the roadway outside the church buildings belongs to a more modern era. Records do not reveal the identity of this phantom peddler but those who have witnessed it say it is spine-chilling experience.

The peddler (referred to as 'paddler' locally) is always encountered at dusk. The phantom bicycle has been carefully described as a black framed type that was popular two generations ago. It features flat handlebars and a distinctive white painted stripe at the bottom of the rear mudguard.

The 'paddler' himself is a ghastly apparition. He is dressed in well worn pitmans' clothes with heavy boots, gloves, and a cap. The face though carries all the marks of death's decay. A lank strand of hair curls down from beneath the cap towards the hollow circles of the vacant eye sockets. The lower jaw sags downwards too, highlighting the whiteness of bone probing its way through grey, shrivelled skin. Blackened teeth rattle within the skull in ghostly harmony with the vibration of the machine.

Beyond the chattering of the teeth and the whirring sound of the wheels, this is said to be a silent spectre. It is also a very sporting one - never creeping up behind unsuspecting pedestrians. The bicycle and it's spectral rider invariably approach the walker head on.

The phenomenon seems unexceptional at first - until the detail of that grizzly countenance imprints itself on the consciousness of the horrified observer. It seems that the observer's eyes are drawn to it as if pulled by a powerful but invisible force. They are compelled to follow it as it passes until the white stripe on the rear guard fades into the pale shadows of evening.

Super-Pit Country

The short journey to Cresswell takes you through the new industrial heartland of this corner of Northumberland. The Alcan factory and the Ellington 'super-pit' are calculated between them to employ half the local workforce.

The old village of Cresswell is beyond new housing developments close to the sea. This is the southern tip of a spectacular seven mile crescent of beach and dunes known as Druridge Bay.

The 14th. century pele tower is within a private walled garden, but it can be clearly seen from the road. The tower is now a roofless ruin encircled by weeds and ivy, but it forms the focus of an interesting supernatural encounter.

For the Love of a Prince

It seems that in Saxon times a lovely daughter of the Cresswell family foolishly gave her heart to a Danish prince. Risking all for the opportunity of escaping 'over the foam' with his loved one the young Dane brought his boat into the bay.

He was intercepted as he stepped ashore and was killed in a brief and bloody skirmish. The young lady had witnessed these events from her vantage point in the tower and was overcome with grief.

Cresswell's Pele Tower

She refused all food, and died in a pitiful state a few days later. Since then 'a wistful white-clad ghost' has often returned to keep vigil on the roof of the old tower.

This particular white lady is a most enduring ghost, who defies the common convention in these things by most frequently being seen during daylight hours. Warm summer evenings seem to provide the best opportunities for a sighting. Serious ghost hunters are recommended to time their arrival in Cresswell accordingly.

Opening Times :

Tynemouth Castle and Priory :	Open standard D.O.E. opening hours.
Seaton Delaval Hall :	Open May-September, Mondays, Wednesdays, and Bank Holidays. 2 p.m - 6 p.m.
Woodhorn Colliery Museum :	Opening hours are presently subject to revision.
Woodhorn Church :	Open Tuesday-Saturday. 10 a.m - noon, 1 p.m - 4 p.m.

No.4 - Kings and Castles

This motoring tour takes about ten hours

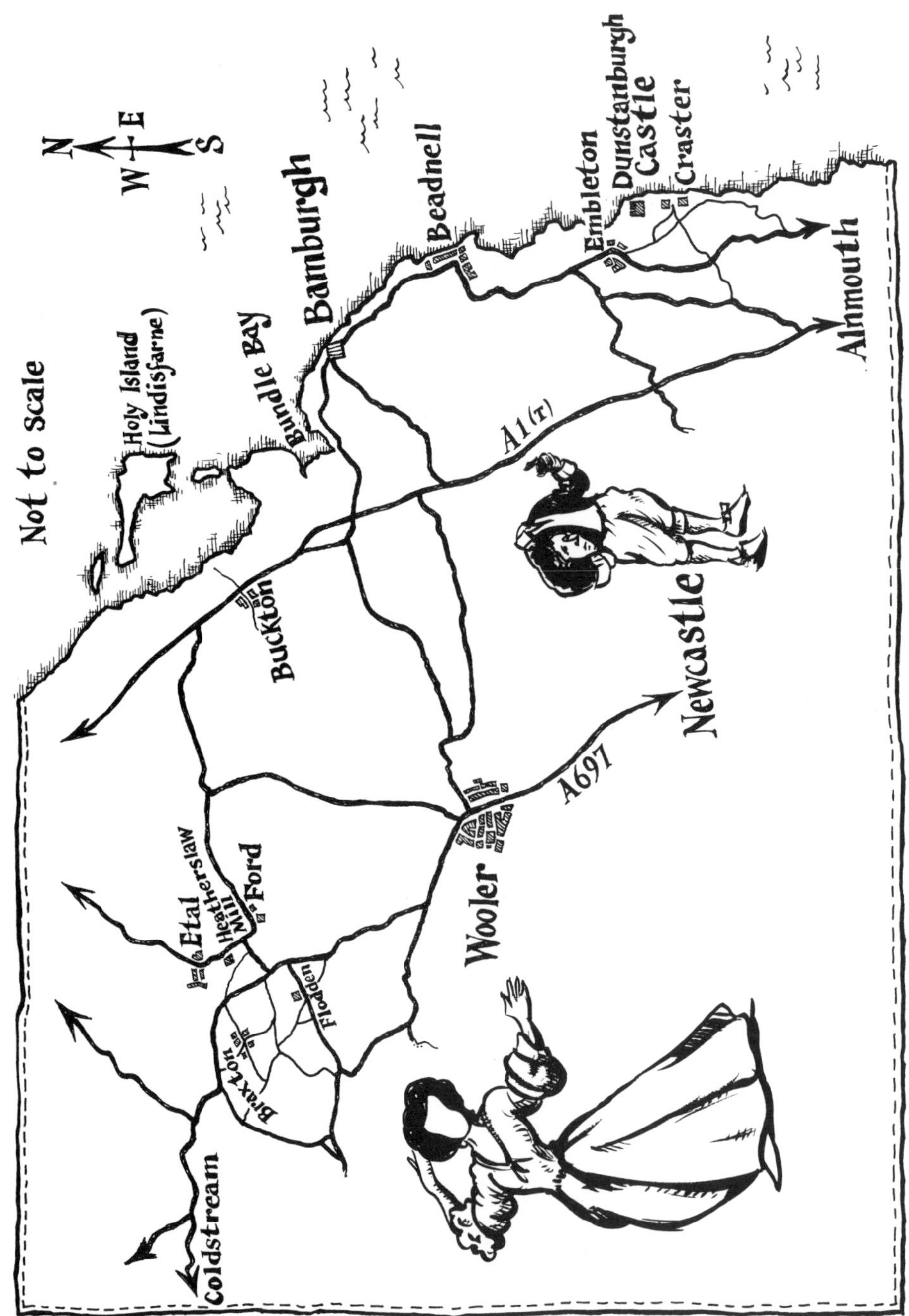
Not to Scale
N
W
E
S
Holy Island (Lindisfarne)
Budle Bay
Bamburgh
Beadnell
Embleton
Dunstanburgh Castle
Craster
Alnmouth
A1(T)
Buckton
Newcastle
A697
Wooler
Etal
Heatherslaw Mill
Ford
Flodden
Branxton
Coldstream

The Classic Tour

For visitors who are lucky enough to be visiting Northumberland for the first time this is the classic tour. The coastline that you will follow for most of the journey cannot be surpassed for drama and beauty, and the contrast provided by the 'model village' of Ford, and the wildness of Flodden Field will never be forgotten.

Dunstanburgh is reached from either Craster or Embleton. The ideal would be to have two cars because both short routes are delightful. The one and a half mile walk from the ancient fishing village of Craster provides impressive coastal scenery with rocks of the Great Whin Sill rising in columns from the sea bed. The path, which leaves Craster from the north, follows the cliff-line to Dunstanburgh, passing the tiny islands of Little Carr and Muckle Carr.

From Embleton village minor roads lead to the golf course, and to footpaths on Embleton Bay, with the coastal footpath continuing to Dunstanburgh Castle.

The Shadow on the Tower

The late 14th. century Embleton Tower was created by a vicar who thought it prudent to fortify his residence. In 1384 the church and vicarage had been badly damaged by Scottish raiders who 'lay in the fields of Embleton and did great destruction'. The same vicar advised villagers to remove the roofs from their homes to create a ruined appearance that would deter future raiders. Records do not reveal whether or not the parishioners of Embleton complied with this request.

At nightfall a curious effect can be observed on the old tower wall. The large shadow of a cross is thrown upon it from the grave of a former vicar. It is said, predictably perhaps, that this symbol of Christianity is to ward off evil spirits who like to 'begin their mischief' at dusk.

The Age of Grave Robbers

Another possibility is that the shadow, which can be frequently seen by moonlight, was intended to discourage the work of resurrectionists. During the early years of the 19th. century the demand for cadavers for dissection by medical students reached its zenith. As the value of a corpse declined rapidly with decomposition, fresh graves were often guarded. But the trade was so valuable that resurrectionists were prepared to take risks.

The most famous exponents of this were Burke and Hare who supplied bodies to anatomists in Edinburgh. They supplemented their 'churchyard stock' with their own murder victims. After turning King's evidence, William Hare admitted that he had 'combined with William Burke to cause the death of 15 persons.' The real number is unknown, but 50 is likely to be nearer the mark.

A Long and Violent History

Dunstanburgh Castle appears to some to be more of an unfinished building site than a ruin. The castle, which stands alone on a small hilltop, was once a virtually impregnable fortress built by Thomas, Earl of Lancaster, in 1313.

Initially the castle was regarded as an 'insurance policy' against Scottish incursions, but after 1340, as the property of John of Gaunt, it became a Lancastrian stronghold in the Wars of the Roses. In 1462 Margaret of Anjou (Queen of Henry VI) lay siege to the castle unsuccessfully. The same Margaret was defeated by Warwick's forces at the Battle of Hexham two years later and the castle, which had already suffered artillery bombardments, was allowed to fall into ruin.

There is a tradition that Queen Margaret escaped from the carnage of the Battle of Hexham and sought temporary refuge at Dunstanburgh before escaping in a boat from the tiny 'Dunstanburgh Port' next to the castle. The port is referred to more than once in history and part of Henry VIII's fleet once sheltered here in a storm.

The site seems inadequate, unless the land level was once considerably lower, and it is possible that 'Dunstanburgh Port', was never a port at all. The respected historian, Robert Hughill, believes it is likely that 'Dunstanburgh Port' was actually at Craster. Nevertheless the tiny inlet in the rocks to the south of the castle is still known as Queen Margaret's Cove.

The main entrance faces to the south. Approaching from Craster we see the great round tower flanking the gateway, and a long high length of curtain wall stretching to the right as far as a tower at the very edge of the cliff. This tower is 'Queen Margaret's Tower', and it is here that the ghost of the weeping Queen still puts in an occasional appearance. Tradition has it that her tears are for those slain at Hexham.

The Spectre in Black Mourning

The spectre is said to cut a striking figure : tall, but 'severe of visage', she is clothed in the black of mourning. The spirit has been seen both at the parapet of the tower and ascending the staircase. A 'unnatural chill breeze' provides an overture to her appearances and an invisible voice intones the name 'Henry'.

Which Henry?

It has been assumed that the call is addressed to the departed spirit of Henry VI. The king regained the monarchy - in 1470 - but died in the Tower of London 'of pure displeasure and melancholy' in May 1471. Shakespeare has him murdered by Richard, Duke of Gloucester (later Richard III). What is certain is that his demise was politically expedient for King Edward IV, whose second reign ended at Westminster in 1483, and whose sons - Edward V and Richard of York - are best remembered as the 'Princes in the Tower'.

Henry VI had always suffered 'a weakness of the brain' and by the year of his death was said to have become a total imbecile. He had been little more than a pawn in the political game for years and it is unlikely that his queen was particular upset by his passing.

A more likely candidate for 'Henry' could be Henry Beaufort, Duke of Somerset. This Henry had been Margaret's confidante and possibly her lover for many years. He was captured after the Battle of Hexham and paid the price of defeat by facing the deadly blow of the axeman in the town market place.

The Bungling Axeman

Another restless spirit at Dunstanburgh is that of the same Thomas, Earl of Lancaster who created it. Thomas had a romantic disposition and was steeped in ancient lore. His intention at Dunstanburgh was to recreate the days of King Arthur by raising on these rocks a second Joyous Garde.

Through 'o'erweening ambition', and a measure of political misjudgement, he came into conflict with another King (Edward II) and was executed in the hall of Pontefract Castle. The executioner was apparently a substitute axeman who took eleven blows to complete what should have been achieved in two or three at the most. It is recorded that even battle-hardened soldiers fainted during the proceedings.

A Macabre Spectre

Consequently the ghost of Earl Thomas is not a pleasing sight. The Victorian ghost hunter, Alfred Dunn, describes the spectre as having 'a singularly macabre appearance with the neck appearing from the blood-splattered shirt in a variety of jagged contours. The head is purchased beneath the arm with the face uppermost. It is a face that is much contorted with the agony of death.'

Those seeking to avoid this grizzly apparition should be warned that it is associated with a number of areas within the castle precincts. These include the wall close to the Postern (Lilburn's) Tower, the fragmentary ruins of the Constable's House, and the Inner Bailey.

It may be little consolation to the spirit of Earl Thomas, but Edward II, who imprisoned him, also suffered a horrible fate at the hands of sadistic murderers at Berkeley Castle in Gloucestershire in 1327.

The Mystery of the Crystal Tomb

There is an unusual story from a later period associated with Dunstunburgh. A favoured version of this tells of a mysterious Knight, Sir Guy, who came riding to the partly ruined castle on the night of a torrential storm. The noise of wind and rain made it impossible for him to be heard and he was forced to shelter in the porch by the gate. At midnight the great doors opened and a huge bearded spectral figure clothed in black beckoned him into the castle.

He was taken to a long arched room which contained a crystal tomb. Within the tomb he could see a beautiful maiden guarded by a hundred sleeping knights. Two giant skeletons stood beside the tomb, one holding a sword and the other a horn.

The brave Sir Guy unwisely took the horn and blew it. The knights began to stir uneasily and the room filled with the acrid smell of rotting flesh. Sir Guy was quickly escorted away by his spectral companion and soon found himself outside the castle walls again huddled up in the porch.

In the morning the storm abated and Sir Guy banged on the wooden doors until he was heard and admitted. His host listened sympathetically to the chronicle of events and told him that there was a local legend about the sleeping Guinevere, Arthur's knights, and Merlin's spell that locked them all in a crystal tomb. If only Sir Guy had chosen the sword, rather than the horn, then the spell would have been broken forever.

By tradition Sir Guy spent the rest of his days seeking the crystal tomb. On his death he was buried nearby, and his ghost continues to play a solitary game of hide and seek amongst the castle ruins.

As Dunstanburgh Castle was built, then haunted, by an Earl with a penchant for recreating a fragment of the Arthurian legend, it is a fine coincidence that it should acquire a second wandering apparition whose eternal mission is to find Guinevere's crystal tomb.

A Popular Village

Beadnell Village is a pleasing place to visit. It is worth driving the half mile or so to the small harbour at Benthall. Here you can climb to a platform on the lime kilns which provides rewarding views over Beadnell Bay to Dunstanburgh. The short walk to the point at Ebb's Nook, passing the fragmentary remains of a 13th. century chapel, offers spectacular views towards the Farne Islands and the famous Longstone Lighthouse.

The Tale of the Ancient Mariner

Mr. David Michelson, once a regular Beadnell visitor, recalls a vivid ghostly experience that occurred here.

" *I was walking with my labrador dog, Blackie, late on one summer's evening in 1958 when I heard a cry coming from the rocks below. At first I thought this must be the call of a seabird so I ignored it. But Blackie was agitated began barking at something that I couldn't see.*"

" *At first there seemed to be nothing more than the breakers crashing against the stacks, but then I saw the head of a man in the water. I won't forget the horrible weeping gash that ran down the side of his cheek to the jaw or the long hair tied into a ponytail. He raised a hand in the air and I thought he might catch hold of a rock, but a surge of water pushed him away again.*"

"*I tried to climb down, but it was very dangerous. I'd not got far when I realised that I'd lost him. I climbed back up, and decided to go for help. Blackie was whimpering loudly and I knew that what I'd seen was somehow not right. It was to do with the face of the man in the water. It was not the face of a modern swimmer or diver. He had the look of the mariner about him, and an ancient mariner at that.*"

" *I reported it of course and made enquiries. Nobody was missing and no body was found. When you tell a story like that you suddenly find out that you're not the only one to have had the experience. The common features are always the gashed face and the ponytail. I know what I saw was there, but it was not of our time. I believe it was the ghost of some poor devil who'd been shipwrecked off the coast there. Heavens knows there are enough candidates for that.* "

" *It was more than a year before I walked out towards the point again. Blackie remembered the exact spot where we had seen the drowning man. He barked at the waves and then set up an awful kind of howling the the like of which I'd never heard from him before. It made me feel faint and sick. I'll never go back. The place is definitely haunted.* "

Beadnell claims to be the best sailing and skin-diving centre in Northumberland and so the village has grown well beyond the original huddle of houses around the church and green.

An Unknown White Lady

The Craster Arms is an 18th. century coaching inn that contains the remains of a pele tower. The most promising site for ghost hunting though is the nearby Beadnell House recently restored as a Hotel.

Mr. Paul Hopper, a former owner of Beadnell House, was uncertain of the identity of the 'white lady' who is seen from time to time drifting around the building. But this particular spectre has established good haunting credentials over the years. Unfortunately there is no story of any credence that establishes her identity, or provides good cause for her ghostly presence.

About midway on the road between Beadnell and Seahouses you will find Monk's House neatly sandwiched between the beach and the road. This 'House on the Shore' (now a small complex of buildings divided into flats) stands on the site of an ancient mill and grain store once owned by the monks of Lindisfarne.

Saints and Shipwrecks

On the beach in front of the house the Clashope Burn runs into the sea between the Monk's House and Shoreston Rocks. This is the very place, according to legend, where a shipwrecked Viking warrior was brought ashore after he had been rescued by a mermaid.

Seahouses has the obvious tourist attractions of a small coastal town and a picturesque fishing harbour. It is also the embarkation point for trips to the Farne Islands.

Legend says that when St. Cuthbert, Bishop of Lindisfarne, came to live on Inner Farne in the 7th. century he put to flight the evil spirits that frequented the place. Naturally enough they only retreated as far as the outer islands. Their hideously deformed, dark-featured wraiths are reputed to enjoy riding on long-horned goats.

When roused in anger they create a cacophony of blood-curdling screams and loud lamenting groans. Some argue that this appalling racket has nothing to do with evil spirits at all, but it is in fact created by the tormented ghosts of drowned sailors. There is little doubt that these noises are common enough on the islands. By an odd coincidence they seem to be most commonly heard during the seabird breeding season.

A Famous Landmark

There is nothing in Britain more evocative of the past than Bamburgh Castle. It is the most prominent landmark in Northumbria and the most spectacular. The castle, seen perhaps to the best advantage from the fine sandy beach, has formed a dramatic setting for countless movies, television dramas and advertising campaigns. In several of the films the castle has played a more convincing role than the actors.

Visiting the interior is perhaps disappointing because a large portion of the building is private accommodation. Nevertheless there are some interesting features, especially in the Great Hall, Armoury, and the neatly organised Museum.

The History of a Mighty Fortress

Bamburgh's history parallels that of Northumbria. The 'craggy citadel' has better claims than Dunstanburgh to be Joyous Garde. Sir Thomas Malory, whose 15th. century 'Morte D'Arthur' firmly transplanted the French legends to these shores, suggested that Bamburgh was the site Sir Lancelot's famous fortress.

What is absolutely certain is that Bamburgh was already a royal centre when Ida, King of Bernicia, and his son, the terrible 'Flamebearer' made it their capital in A.D. 547.

Ida's grandson, Ethelfrith, joined Bernicia with Deira to form a united Northumbria - a kingdom much larger than that defined by modern boundaries.

Although York became the Kingdom's capital, Bamburgh was an important royal residence and many of the early kings were crowned here.

The golden age of Bamburgh began in the 7th. century when the castle fell by conquest into the hands of the King Edwin. He brought the Roman missionary Paulinus to preach Christianity in his lands around Bamburgh. Perhaps this was not totally appreciated because he was defeated and murdered by pagan enemies at Hatfield (near Doncaster) in A.D. 633.

Edwin was succeeded by Oswald, son of his old enemy Ethelfrith who has founded the Northumbrian Kingdom. Oswald set up the monastery on Lindisfarne that was to become one of the greatest centres of art and learning in Europe.

The decline in Bamburgh's importance began with the Norse attack of A.D. 933. When the mighty warrior Eric Bloodaxe was killed at Stainmore (A.D. 956) Northumbria was joined to the English Kingdom of King Edred.

Bamburgh Castle

Bamburgh was attacked by Norsemen again in 1015, and was besieged by William 11 (Rufus). It was around this time that an important relic was stolen. This was King Oswald's remarkably preserved arm and hand which had been kept in a silver casket in the tiny St.Peter's chapel.

The castle, if not the relic, was restored by Henry 1 but it suffered two more lengthy sieges during the Wars of the Roses.

By the 17th. century it had become dilapidated but was restored by Lord Crewe, Bishop of Durham. In 1894 it was purchased by the first Lord Armstrong, whose family are still the owners.

Green Jane - The Falling Phantom

No castle in history has enjoyed a longer, or more varied and violent career. Surprisingly it does not seem to be particularly well haunted, but there is at least one rather special ghost.

Viewing the castle from the green there is a stairway that winds up the steep cliff to a small postern gate north of the clock tower. From time to time a woman's figure in a hooded cloak will appear in front of the gate. In her arms she carries a small bundle wrapped in cloth. As she begins her descent towards the green it appears as if she stumbles and falls. She cries out in alarm as she falls down the steep narrow stairway and disappears from view.

From somewhere above her there is a hollow ring of laughter.

Several visitors to Bamburgh have reported this event. On each occasion they have rushed up the flights of steps to aid the stricken woman. Never has a trace been found of the lady or her bundle.

It is a singular and recurring story that is told with little variation as to detail. There is much discussion about the 'identify' of the 'Falling Phantom', but one story seems to provide the best explanation.

In the Scottish wars at the time of Henry V Bamburgh suffered greatly. The burgesses (freemen) of the district were recorded as having decreased in number from 120 to 13, and there was a petition for the reduction of rents.

A young woman, known only as Jane, was sent by her impoverished family to the castle to beg for food. Unfortunately the castle guards abused her, refused to allow her to see the Lord, and laughed as they pushed her out of the castle by the postern gate. Weak from hunger and the indignities she had suffered the girl stumbled on the stairway and fell to her death. In her arms she was carrying a baby who also perished in the fall.

The 'Falling Phantom' is sometimes called 'Green Jane' because of the striking colour of her cloak. The same colour that has been reported by those who have seen the apparition.

The Legend of the Laidley Worm

Perhaps the most popular legend associated with Bamburgh is that of the Laidley Worm.

It is said that long ago the daughter of a King of Northumbria had been turned into a dragon (or 'worm') by the wicked Queen, her stepmother. The King was blissfully unaware that the Queen was a witch, and had married the woman as comfort for his old age.

The Laidley Worm laid waste the country for miles around, until at last the king's own son - The Childe of Wynde - volunteered to fight the beast. Happily, before battle commenced, the dragon revealed her true identity. The 'Childe' was saved the misfortune of combat with his own sister.

The spell was broken and the Laidley Worm turned again from dragon to princess. This pleased everyone, with the likely exception of the wicked stepmother whose opinion was never asked because she had already turned into a toad and hopped away into a cave beneath the castle. In the best traditions of folklore she remains there until this day.

It is said that a door into the cave opens briefly every seventh Christmas Eve. Any brave warrior is then at liberty to enter. If he is able to unsheath the Childe of Wynde's sword three times, and to blow three times on the great horn, he then only has to kiss the toad in order to win the eternal gratitude of the witch-queen, who will be fully restored to her normal form.

Perhaps it may be unwise to accept this challenge. The witch-queen was a powerful lady with dark, uncertain moods. It would be a poor reward for for such kindness to find oneself turned, like the princess, into a dragon. It is also worth considering that laying waste to land around Bamburgh is a contravention of bye-laws which forbid the lighting of open fires, even on the beach. It's no fun being a dragon any more.

The castle is an important reminder of what an important place Bamburgh once was. By the 19th. century, when it had become no more than the delightful seaside village it is today, it briefly became once more the focus of the nation's attention.

The Darling of Victorian England

Grace Horsley Darling was the daughter of the lighthouse keeper at Longstone. Together with her father she took out a small boat (a coble) to rescue the survivors of the wrecked steamship Forfarshire.

This single event in September 1838 made Grace Darling the heroine of the age. The story gathered ever more elaborate detail as it developed from one publication to the next. Grace was celebrated in song and verse, given a gold medal, awarded a treasury grant, and became quite wealthy through a public subscription fund.

The rescue had demonstrated exemplary courage. Grace and her father knew when they set out in the coble that they would be unable to return without the assistance of the shipwrecked crew. They took the risk without hesitation.

The degree of fame and fortune that Grace Darling achieved had much to do with what we would now call 'media hype'. She had all the essential qualities of a idealised Victorian heroine - bravery, frailty, innocence, and youth. Grace died of consumption in 1842 at the age of twenty-seven. Her early death caused writers' inkwells to be emptied. emptied a second time. Bamburgh for years afterwards became almost a place of pilgrimage.

Grace Darling's canopied memorial can be found in St. Aidan's churchyard. Because of erosion, the original effigy was removed a hundred years ago and can be found in the church. It is a sign of the times perhaps that the replacement stone carving is now more worn than the original. The heroine is buried in the family plot nearby.

The tiny Grace Darling museum is a more satisfactory memorial and it is well worth a visit. It includes the coble (rowing boat) which was used for the Forfarshire rescue.

Unusual Relics

St. Aidan's Church contains other unusual relics. It is said that the saint died in the unusually long chancel (the site of the earlier Saxon church) on August 31st. A.D. 652. A beam against which the saint rested as he breathed his last has twice survived major fires in the church. It is now incorporated into the roof below the tower. It serves no structural purpose and it is assumed that it has been placed in its present position for safe keeping. Bede's chronicle suggests that fragments of the beam were stolen for their healing properties.

Another surprising feature of the church is the 13th. century vaulted crypt which was discovered when some decayed oak planks were removed from the chancel floor in 1837. This crypt was possibly built for the safe keeping and display of relics - possibly these of St. Aidan. A wall into which a small Saxon sun-dial has been inserted divides the crypt into two compartments.

Another Heroine - Dorothy Forster

When the crypt was discovered five coffins lay on the stone shelf at the east end. These contained the bones of celebrated members of Bamburgh's Forster family.

One was Ferdinando Forster who was murdered in the streets of Newcastle in 1701.

Another was General Thomas Forster who was a leader of the Jacobite rising in 1715. He surrendered to the King's forces at Preston and was taken to London's notorious Newgate Prison to stand trial.

Three days before the trial he was rescued from the prison and escaped to Boulogne. The dramatic and daring escape was arranged, according to Walter Beasant's popular novel, by his sister. Indeed it is likely that Dorothy Forster played some part in the escape, but her role may have been less important than the novel suggests.

Whatever the truth is, the event gave her such acclaim that her 'heroine status' in Northumbria is only slightly below that of Grace Darling. It is strange coincidence that her final resting place should be the crypt of St. Aidan's Church, just a few yards from the Grace Darling Memorial.

From Budle Bay to Buckton

The road from Bamburgh sweeps past Budle Bay. This can appear either as delightful blue dinghy-sailing waters, or unimpressive mud flats according to the tide. Beyond the bay it is possible to pick out a number of rocky crags to the left (south) of the road. One of these is the Spindlestone, a whinstone pillar, which according to legend is the place where the Childe of Wynde tethered his horse before going to do battle with the Laidley Worm.

The tiny hamlet of Buckton is a couple of hundred yards west of the A1. At first sight it seems that there is little of interest here apart from the farm and manor house, a walled garden, an ancient lime kiln, and pleasing views over Lindisfarne and towards the Kyloe Hills.

An Improbable Haunting

Most of the trees that surrounded the buildings and spread towards the A1 have disappeared. It is said that one of the clumps of trees (but infuriatingly there is no clear evidence which) is known as Grizzel's Clump - supposedly the favoured haunt of an interesting but improbable ghost.

In July 1685, Sir John Cochrane lay in an Edinburgh prison under sentence of death for his part in the Duke of Argyll's rising against James II. As the warrant of execution travelled north Sir John's daughter, Grizzel, disguised herself as a man and hid amongst the trees. She held up the mail coach seized the post bag that contained the warrant.

Her efforts delayed the execution long enough for Sir John's friends to arrange for his pardon and Grizzel fortunately was not held to account for the robbery. Nevertheless her ghost is reputed to haunt the appropriate spot.

Research has so far revealed no further details of this unlikely apparition. It is possible that the 'ghost' has been 'created' through the association of the clump and a celebrated crime. But could there be a completely different reason for a genuine haunting in this area?

The Phantom Hitchhiker

Some years ago a doctor was driving home along the A1 with a medical colleague. The car headlights picked out a young woman hiker in the mist at the road side. The doctor stopped, wound down the window, and asked if he could help. The woman pointed towards some trees and the mangled wreckage of a car that had recently left the road before crashing into one of them.

The doctor rushed to the wreckage with the young woman following close behind. Meanwhile his colleague drove away to find a telephone. The doctor could remember few details later about the woman, other than that she had fair hair, wore a cagoule and held a rucksack in her arms. She had been shaking and unable to speak - classic symptoms he thought of shock.

It was the car that demanded his attention first. Inside was a man who had serious head injuries. Happily he was still alive and the doctor administered emergency first aid. Minutes later an ambulance arrived and the man was rushed to hospital.

It was only now that the doctor remembered the lady hiker. His searching proved fruitless. She had vanished in the darkness.

The injured man survived the accident. He said later that he had been travelling alone in the darkness when a young woman stepped into the road in front of him. He had swerved to avoid her but felt a sickening crunch as she fell beneath his wheels. He lost control of the car and ran headlong into the trees.

The mysterious hiker was never found. The car was carefully examined. There was nothing to suggest that it had hit anything other than the trees.

Perhaps the matter would have remained a mystery but for a genuinely strange coincidence. Records reveal that there had been one previous accident at the spot, when a woman had been killed by a speeding motorist. The incident had taken place just a year to the day previously. The unfortunate woman had been a Scandinavian tourist, who had been dropped near the spot after hitching a ride from outside Edinburgh. Her description matched exactly that given by the doctor.

The Lindisfarne Causeway

Care should be taken when crossing to Lindisfarne (Holy Island), because tides make it inaccessible twice each day. Safe crossing times are displayed at the start of the causeway, but it is better to plan arrival and departure times well in advance. Tourist Information Centres and the local press publish crossing times, or you can rely on tide tables which can be purchased in Seahouses, Alnwick, Berwick, and at the island's post office.

It is recommended that you do not attempt to cross between two hours prior to high tide and three and a half hours afterwards. If you are relying on tide tables remember to allow for British Summer Time.

It is surprising perhaps that despite all warnings there are several vehicles trapped by the rising water each year, and soggy motorists have to climb to the sanctuary of the refuges. It is an uncomfortable, expensive, and embarrassing experience.

For most visitors to Lindifarne though the experience is one of sheer delight. The island provides remarkable value in accommodation and a warm welcome for the visitor.

It is a very special place steeped with the aura of history and legend. Stepping stones, marked by stakes close to the motorists causeway, mark the 11th. century Pilgrim's Way. Lindisfarne still creates the same spirit of tranquillity and reflection that visitors have been enjoying for a very long time.

In the Footsteps of Pilgrims

Lindisfarne became the cradle of Celtic Christianity in Northumbria after King Oswald (who had been raised by the monks of Iona) invited the Irish monk Aidan to bring the Christian message to Bernicia.

St. Aidan's Statue, Lindisfarne

Aidan chose the island for his monastic community which began in A.D. 635. Oswald died in battle at Oswestry in A.D. 642. but his head was returned to the island and became its first sacred relic. His severed arm and hand of course were kept at Bamburgh. In a way this bizarre division of relics symbolised the early unity of Kingdom and Church, and the extent of their inter-dependence.

It was relics again, those of St. Cuthbert, that were to have a lasting and profound effect on the community.

Like St. Aidan before him Cuthbert preferred the life of a hermit on Inner Farne to the pastoral obligations of a Bishop's See. Indeed it took the king and a company of monks begging him on their knees before he reluctantly accepted the responsibility.

Cuthbert became bishop in A.D. 685, but foretelling his own death he returned to Inner Farne two years later. He was buried in St. Peter's Church in March A.D. 687.

Eleven years later the monks dug up the remains and were amazed to find that the body had not decayed. The monks kept the relics in a specially prepared reliquary coffin and the cult of this popular saint began. Over a century later a Viking raid forced the monks to find a safer place for themselves and the relics. These were transported to Norham, Chester-le-Street, and finally to Durham. Parts of the coffin and other objects associated with the saint are still preserved in Durham Cathedral.

It was mainly because of St. Cuthbert's shrine that the island became a popular pilgrimage and burial place. The monastery became very wealthy through attracting generous benefactors - such as King Ceowulf - who retired as a monk here in A.D. 737.

Of course such fame and wealth attracted unwelcome visitors. In the Viking raid of A.D. 793 most of the island's inhabitants were savagely murdered. The church and parts of the monastery were left in ruins and the surviving monastic community began the series of moves (carrying the relics) which was to end in Durham two hundred years later.

Strangely enough St. Cuthbert's relics were deposited once more on the island in the eleventh century as Anglo-Saxon clerics fled from Durham after the Norman Conquest. When the situation became 'safe' they were returned forever to Durham.

This chronicle of the travelling relics demonstrates the devotion of the monks and Christian community of Northumbria to their saint. It was a devotion born of mystery and miracles that has meant that for a thousand years Lindisfarne has also been 'Holy Island'. It is still very much a source of spiritual strength to people who return to the island year after year. The casual visitor should be mindful of, and respect this.

The Lindisfarne Museum

The fabulous illuminated manuscripts known as the Lindisfarne Gospels were probably prepared for the enshrinement of St. Cuthbert in A.D. 698. They are now in the care of the British Museum, but there is an excellent facsimile in the church. The museum houses imaginative displays of artifacts and excellent displays tell the story of the island's history. It is perhaps the best small museum in Northumbria.

The island's ghosts are not all associated with its ancient monuments.

Saint Cuthbert is said to walk along the shore close to the tiny island named after him.

A Ghastly Face

At the nearby coastguard station there is a mysterious and horrific face that appears at the window some twenty feet or so above ground level. It is a shrivelled, half-skeletal face with a ghastly green complexion and an irregular matting of lank black hair. The face seems fixed in a stare, yet there are no eyes - only the lifeless sunken orbs of the skull.

There has been much speculation about this sinister spectre. Some believe that it is a disembodied head cast aside after the robbery of a grave. Others suggest it is the tormented spirit of a heathen invader struck by a bolt of lightning after he had shamelessly murdered a monk. Neither of these are satisfactory explanations.

A better theory is that this ghastly apparition is a kind of reflection. There have been thousands of shipwrecks recorded around the Farne Islands and it was not uncommon at one time to find a partly decomposed corpse washed ashore. The coastguard was generally the first to be alerted when a corpse was found.

Many years ago one young coastguard became so distressed by the unpleasant duty of removing a body from the water that he began to suffer terrible nightmares. One night he woke up screaming, rose from his bed and ran to the coastguard station. All efforts to calm him failed, and in his hallucinations and delusions he swore that he could see the dreadful face of the man pulled from the water staring at him through the darkened glass of the window.

Could it be that the vivid image in that young man's tortured mind is somehow forever etched in the ether? Do receptive eyes and minds still pick this out as a kind of reflection in the glass?

It is a wild and improbable explanation, but it is also strangely believable.

In the Picture

The Priory is a ruined 12th. century building built on the site of the 7th. century church that contained St. Cuthbert's shrine. From time to time the image of a 'white monk' appears on photographs taken of the archway that is now the visitor's entrance to the priory.

Nobody knows who this photogenic (but otherwise invisible) monk may be, and there is no history of more traditional hauntings at The Priory.

Lindisfarne Priory and Castle

The Petting Stone

Close to the priory is the 12th. century St. Mary's Church. The remaining parts of the original structure were cunningly disguised by Victorian restoration work.

Links with the island's past have been rather better preserved in the churchyard where there is the curious petting stone. After the wedding ceremony new brides leap over the stone. Their future good fortune is measured by their athletic performance in performing this feat. It is rumoured that modern brides are inclined to cheat by having two men lift them high over the stone.

Lindisfarne Castle

Lindisfarne Castle, like Dunstunburgh and Bamburgh, is perched on a rocky mound. It was built around 1550 from stone conveniently provided by the ruined monastery. It withstood a Parliamentary siege during the civil war and was occupied by Jacobite rebels in 1715.

By the turn of the present century it had fallen into disrepair. The owner of 'Country Life' magazine, Edward Hudson, purchased the property and commissioned the architect Sir Edward Lutyens to supervise the restorations. The present luxurious gentleman's residence, completed in 1903, is now in the care of the National Trust.

The capturing of the castle in 1715 is a bizarre story which may provide the background for strange occurrences that are reported from time to time at the castle.

A Phantom Custodian

A fanatical Jacobite, Lancelot Errington, and his nephew took the castle for the Pretender by trickery.

It seems that the castle's garrison consisted of an elderly gunner and a sentinel. The gunner practised the barbering trade in his off-duty hours and Errington presented himself as a customer. Later he returned with his nephew to 'look for the key to his watch'. When the door was opened he thrust a pistol into the barber's face and held him captive. After a brief struggle the sentinel was also subdued. The 'garrison' were disarmed and pushed out of the castle.

For several days Errington and his nephew held the castle expecting Jacobite forces to arrive from the mainland. In the event it was king's men who landed on the island and the two Jacobites were bundled off to Berwick goal. Their further adventures included burrowing their way out of the goal, hiding for nine days in a pea-sack at Bamburgh, and escaping to the continent in a small boat.

Fishing Boats and Lindisfarne Castle

It is said that keys can turn in locks in the castle without the agency of any human hand. Doors and windows will sometimes open and close seemingly of their own accord. There is no explanation for this.

Some people believe that the mysterious force behind these events is the now vigilant veteran gunner who has returned to the scene of his humiliation. Is he making occasional tours of the castle, diligently checking ever door and window for security against those who may wish to enter illegally?

Visitors are therefore advised to make sure they have valid tickets before entering. After all, the old gunner is best remembered for his skill with the cutthroat razor...

A Mysterious Event

One curious tale has been told by a 'courting couple' who had parked one evening on a grassy bank not far from the castle. It was a beautiful summer's evening, but the couple had little interest either in the glow of the sunset or the magnificent darkening profile of the castle. Their thoughts were entirely focused on the natural, rather than the supernatural.

Suddenly they were aware of a loud rumbling noise which came from above the car roof. The noise sounded like chains being dragged down a flight of stone stairs and lasted for just a few seconds.

Although they both heard it they were engaged in such frenzied activity of their own that neither said anything. Some minutes later the strange noise was repeated but this time it was very much louder. The sound was also more distinct now - it sounded like the thunder of horses' hooves.

They wiped the condensation from the car's rear window and peered out cautiously. There was nothing to be seen.

By now the magic of romance had evaporated. A chill, described as an icy blast, seemed to surround them. The young man got out of the vehicle and looked around. A similar but remoter noise seemed to be coming from somewhere near the castle. He listened for a few moments and realised the sound was increasing in intensity. Whatever was creating the disturbance was heading straight towards the car.

" *I was paralysed with fear,* " he said, " *and could only listen and watch. It was definitely horses ; the sound was most distinct. Now I could see the cloud of dust they were kicking up, but whatever created it was invisible.* "

"*My girlfiend was suddenly tugging at my arm and pushing me back towards the car. I tried to start the engine but it was dead. The starter motor just refused to engage. All the time the noise was getting louder and louder. I put my hands over my ears and it seemed that my brain could explode with the pain of that volume of noise. The cold was now dreadful and I was shivering and shaking like a leaf. Just when I thought I could stand no more the sound began to pass by. It moved slowly at first, and then more rapidly. Suddenly it was silent. The silence seemed very strange."*

" Then the temperature changed. From being icy cold it was suddenly warm again. I could feel the throbbing pain of circulation returning to my fingers and wrists. When I turned the ignition switch the engine fired first time."

" I honestly don't know what happened and I've never heard a decent explanation. People have talked about phantom coaches, but it really wasn't that. I can only describe it as a supernatural stampede. Whatever was out there was invisible, but very real. It's not something I'd like to experience again."

" We've had to put up with a lot of teasing. You know, things like 'did the earth move for you?' But I can tell you it wasn't funny at the time. I can still feel the way that every hair on my neck stood to attention, and that awful biting chill. It was the weirdest thing you can imagine."

Ford Castle

An almost inescapable twinge of sadness felt when leaving the island probably explains why many vistors return over and over again.

The next part of the route offers few obvious visual delights but the visitor must be assured that the journey to Ford is well worth the effort.

The village itself is delightful, being largely remodelled by Lady Waterford in the late 19th century, but it is the castle that mostly commands our attention. The property which is used by Northumberland County Council for educational courses is not open to the public. The visitor must therefore be content with the view from the road.

The castle was built in 1287 and captured by the Scots in 1385. The invaders, possibly inspired by their success at Bannockburn, decided to demolish large parts of the building.

It was events surrounding the Battle of Flodden (1513) that gave the castle its special place in history.

The owner at the time, Sir William Heron, was held prisoner in Scotland. His young wife asked the English general, the Earl of Surrey, to intercede with the Scot's King - James IV - so that Ford may be spared a second dose of demolition. Two Scottish noblemen were offered in return for the safety of the castle and its inhabitants.

Ford Castle and The King's Tower

James IV was not impressed with either the Earl of Surrey or his offer. He advanced, took Ford, and made it his military headquarters.

An Unusual Conquest

It is said that Lady Heron was determined to buy time for Surrey's expeditionary force by delaying the further advance of the Scots. The tactic she employed was to make advances of her own to King James, who is believed to have found this a bargain more to his liking than the return of two noblemen.

The dalliance that followed was supposed to have been facilitated by a secret staircase that linked their apartments. When the Marchioness of Waterford restored the castle to make it her home a staircase was discovered and there was immediate speculation about its historical significance. Sadly there is good evidence that the staircase was built two and a half centuries after Lady Heron's heroic efforts to improve the English chances of victory.

There is contradictory evidence too as to whether or not King James ever slept at Ford Castle, but the tradition remains that he left reluctantly and wearily on the dawn of the day of battle itself. This may be improbable, although it is recorded that Chatelaine Heron was a remarkably beautiful woman...

There is an inscription in the 'King's Room' (in the tower to the west of the main building) that reads : 'King James ye 4th. of Scotland did lye here at Ford Castle A.D. 1513'. This perhaps goes to prove that people should not believe what they read - even if it is carved in stone.

One thing we know for certain is that when the soldiers left Ford on the fateful road to Flodden Field, King James left instructions that it should be razed to the ground. Presumably this was a military decision, rather than a comment on the standards of comfort offered by the establishment.

The Grey Lady of the King's Tower

The 'King's Tower' has a 'grey lady' apparition. This is often presumed to be the ghost of Lady Heron who was apparently upset when King James decided to burn down the castle after all.

There are said to be 'cold spots' in a number of the castle rooms which cannot be easily explained by the inadequate heating system. 'Cold Spots' are of course a common phenomenon in rooms that are reputed to be haunted. In Ford Castle some of these rooms have also been described by visitors as having 'an oppressive' or even 'unhappy' feel to them.

Certainly the events of 1513, which ended so tragically at Flodden Field, are sufficient to create any number of lost and wandering spirits.

Heatherslaw and Etal

Close to Ford is the recently restored Heatherslaw Mill, one of the oldest water-driven mills in Britain. The original mill, dating from the 13th. century, was largely rebuilt in the 18th. It is open to the public throughout the summer months and is well worth a visit.

On the way to Flodden Field, it is also worth pausing briefly at Etal. The castle here was never rebuilt after it,too, was destroyed by the Scots on the way to Flodden. The castle gatehouse, a massive and gloomy structure, remains quite well preserved. The Keep is a mere shell, but some of its main features are still traceable.

Etal Castle

Flodden Field

The site of the Battle of Flodden Field is about half a mile beyond the village of Branxton. A specially raised platform encourages the visitor to imagine the bloody events of the afternoon of September 9th. 1513.

The Earl of Surrey had been allowed by the Prior of Durham to carry the sacred banner of St. Cuthbert into the battle. It was an important talisman recognised by the soldiers to have protected the English in many previous battles.

The weather was appalling with the armies hardly recognising friend from foe as they took up their formations about half a mile away from each other.

The Scots enjoyed early success. This encouraged James IV to abandon his strong position and to charge down the hill towards the enemy. The steep slippery ground slowed the advance and the Scots suffered heavy casualties through cannon fire and 'a rain of arrows.' Then the English made best use of their superiority in numbers, weaponry and tactics. Their skilled use of the long pike in particular proved decisive.

Two hours later an estimated nine to ten thousand Scots were dead. Casualties were relatively light on the English side.

King James himself was reported to have died bravely, fighting within an isolated and decreasing circle of his guards and noblemen. The butchery that took place during, and after, the battle makes it, perhaps, the most savage ever fought on English soil. It was also the last great medieval battle. Knights would never again fight in heavy armour. Small arms would soon replace swords and spears as the decisive weapons of war.

Sir William Scott and Lord Dacre were instructed to view the body of James IV. The corpse had been stripped bare and a deep wound was cut from ear to ear through the throat. One hand had been severed. Indeed the body was so generally mutilated that it was difficult at first for the gentlemen to be positive about the identification.

The remains were wrapped in the tattered shreds of the Royal Standard and taken to Berwick for embalming. Finally the king was carried in a cart to London and interred in an unmarked grave. More of the dead were buried in pits close to St. Paul's Church at Branxton. Some of these 'pitiful mounds' can still be identified.

A singular phenomenon has been reported by those who walk across the battlefield. Fragments of clothing and brightly coloured pieces of cloth are sometimes seen flapping in the breeze on the gorse. As the visitor approaches more closely they fade and then vanish from view.

There is surely no need to talk of ghosts here.

Flodden Field

Opening Times :

Dunstanburgh Castle :	Open all day throughout the season. Limited winter opening.
Bamburgh Castle :	April - September daily. From 2 p.m.
Grace Darling Museum :	April - October. 11 a.m. - 7 p.m.
Lindisfarne Priory and Museum :	Open Daily.
Lindisfarne Castle :	April - September. 11 a.m. - 1 p.m., 2 p.m. - 5 p.m. Closed Tuesdays and Good Friday.
Heatherslaw Mill :	Open during the summer months.

No.5 - 'Phantoms and Follies'

The circular motoring tour takes about five hours

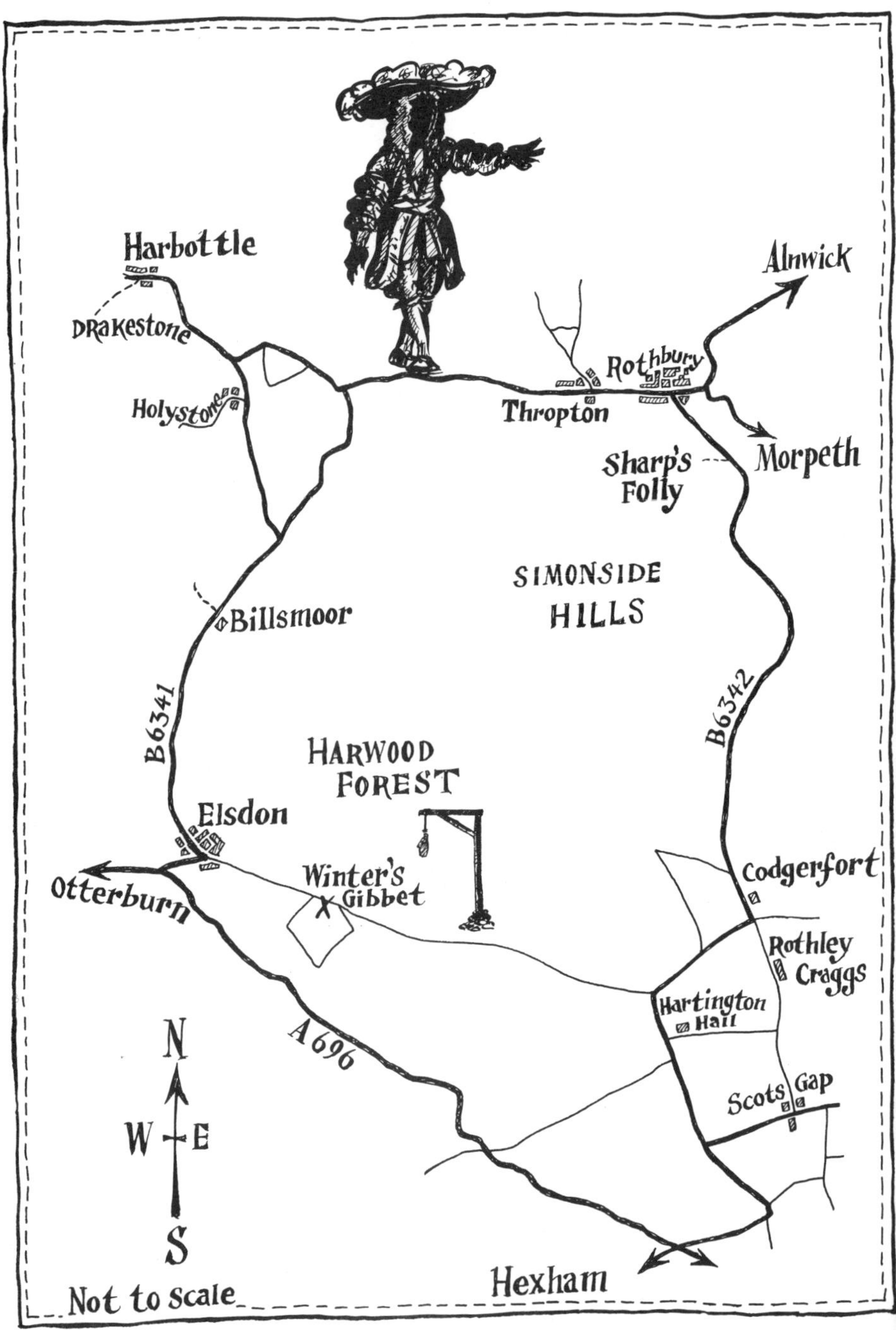
Harbottle
Drakestone
Holystone
Alnwick
Rothbury
Thropton
Morpeth
Sharp's Folly
SIMONSIDE HILLS
Billsmoor
B6341
B6342
HARWOOD FOREST
Elsdon
Otterburn
Winter's Gibbet
Codgerfort
Rothley Craggs
Hartington Hall
A696
Scots Gap
N
W
E
S
Hexham
Not to scale

A Timeless Valley

There is nowhere in England where you feel closer to the mysteries of the past than in the wilds of Northumberland. You can walk all day through fabulous landscapes and not see living soul. The past is all around. Every pile of broken stones has a story to tell.

Rothbury is the capital of Coquetdale. The village is a bustling cheerful place, flanked on one side by a sweeping crescent of trees, and on the other by the dark sinister ridges of the Simonside Hills.

Taking the Hexham road over the Coquet Bridge you climb quickly to Garleigh Moor. A brief diversion brings you to Sharpe's Folly - a tower constructed by a Victorian gentleman determined to catch a glimpse of the sea. You would have more chance at the rear of the Gallowgate Terrace of seeing Newcastle score a goal today. Trees stand with branches raised like the arms of adoring fans in front of the crumbling tower.

Another example of man's folly is seen on the climb to the open moor. A kind of ghostly sentinel, in the shape of a concrete pillbox, stands silently alone - still waiting to defend Coquetdale against the advancing army of the Third Reich.

The Curlew sign shows that the Simonside Hills are incorporated in the National Park. The narrow road runs briefly through plantations, then back to open moor. Two hundred metres beyond the trees a footpath winds up to the Simonside ridges. The sign 'Beware Adders' is a stark reminder of the solitude of this place.

It is worth a brisk five minute walk to the next 'Beware Adders' sign, close to the first group of shooting boxes. Above rise the black Simonside Ridges. It is unwise to go on. You could survive the snakes and the sucking mud of the peat-bogs only to encounter the mischievous and deadly Simonside dwarfs, called Deugars, who live in secret caves and take great pleasure from luring unsuspecting walkers to their doom.

A Legend Begins

On a chill autumn day in 1661, James Hall, a Coquetdale shepherd, stumbled across a pile of charred and broken bones at a place called Selby's Cove below Simonside. At first he was not sure these were human remains as they were scattered and picked almost clean. But as he examined the debris more closely he found the upper portion of a skull. When he turned it over, the broken teeth and hollow eyes greeted him with a hideous grin. He dropped the skull back into the pile and saw it shatter into pieces as if it had been a discarded piece of pottery.

James recalled later that he began to shake and became breathless. It was only with determined resolution that he forced himself to stand in that spot. He looked feverishly around and soon enough his eyes located a smaller skull nearby. He would not pick it up, but already he knew what it meant.

Some weeks before a farmer from Rothley, who held grazing pasture on the high Simonside Moor, had mysteriously disappeared with two of his sons. James remembered that the youngest boy had been about seven years of age.

James surveyed the scene for a minute or two longer but could find no trace of a third skull. What he did notice however were fragments of leather bound closely around bones that perhaps had once formed the junction of an ankle and a foot. Later he spoke of the distinctive foul acid smell of burning peat that seemed to hang in the air around the hollow.

He felt giddy and dry mouthed as the Deugar tales of his childhood flooded back into his consciousness. He remembered only too well the accounts of tricks played by the vile hunchbacked dwarfs that brought a screaming death to their victims as they fell from the precipice. The corpses, he recalled, were slow roasted over a peat fire for the culinary delectation of the murderers.

He had seen enough and tried to turn away, but it seemed as if an invisible force rooted his boots to the ground. Something made him lift his eyes to the crag above and for a moment he was sure he caught sight of the disfigured shape of some stunted half-human creature as it bobbed between the rocks. He said later that he tried to scream but the sound would not pass his lips.

It was the sound of a huntsman's horn that heralded his rescue. Moments later, as if from nowhere, the pack of hounds surrounded him. Horrified he watched as they set upon the bones, cracking, chewing and fighting over the tastiest of them. It seemed an age before the huntsmen arrived to whip them away from their feast. Already it was impossible to say for certain what the origin of the remaining fragments of smoke blackened bone might have been.

What little remained was later gathered up by James and some companions from Rothbury. It is said that the men placed the sorry fragments in sacks and carried them back to the village. Discreet arrangements were made for committal to consecrated ground.

The story of James (also known as 'Jem ') Hall is the best known of the Deugar legends. In case the intrepid ghosthunter may be inspired to set off hurriedly in search of the dwarfs, he should perhaps take note of a second and equally unpleasant story. This has been impossible to place or date accurately, but it is known that it was already in circulation in the early years of the 16th. century.

David Meets the Deugar

The story goes that a young a shepherd boy, David, once followed a lamb across the lonely ridges until it became trapped in a peat bog. The boy understood the peril of entering the bog alone and cast his eyes around the landscape looking for signs of human activity. A pall of smoke caught his attention, so he set off down a steep winding path towards a primitive hut balanced precariously at the edge of the precipice.

The approach to the shelter revealed nothing but darkness behind a faint glow of flames, but a shuffling noise encouraged him to investigate further. As he stepped inside the hut he encountered a hideously ugly creature. This Deugar appears to have been a particularly unpleasant specimen of his type. He had a bulbous turnip-shaped nose and wild staring eyes, and to add to the fearsome impression were more customary Deugar features - blackened teeth, a twisted back and talon-like fingers.

David managed to control his fear and aversion and requested help. The Deugar offered an unusual bargain. If the boy was prepared to build up the meagre fire, the Deugar would make use of a magic spell to free the lamb from the clinging mud.

David agreed and began to grope around the shadowy corners of the hut looking for logs. The aroma of rotting flesh and the chill of a breeze at his feet were ample warnings to him of grave danger. He cleverly used his shepherd's crook to reach and gather logs from the darkest and coldest corners of the shelter, and to toss them on the fire. When the task was complete the Deugar promised the boy that his kindness would be rewarded.

This was obviously a dwarf of principle, and when David reached the high moor he found that the lamb was free. He tucked it under his arm and set off quickly for home as it was now almost dark. As he passed directly above the precipice he could see a brightly burning fire no more than a pace or two from the edge of the cliff below. But the shelter and its hideous inhabitant had vanished.

Deugar hunting has recently become popular, and mountain bikes can be specially hired in Rothbury for this purpose. Expedition leaders, Shaun and Richard Irving, are expert bikers with thorough knowledge of the hills. They are also knowledgeable in Deugar-craft and have yet to lose anyone under their protection.

Many attempts to track the Deugars to their lair have failed, but there are several accounts of sightings in recent years. Two young men from Ambleside have recently offered one plausible explanation.

A Brocken Spectre

Chris Banting and Simon Lee are experienced hill walkers. Their visit to Coquetdale however was their first encounter with the infamous Simonside Ridge.

What they observed was a Brocken Spectre. This one was huge and surrounded by a vivid halo of colour. The enlarged twisted shape might easily have been mistaken for a hunchback which is an important Deugar characteristic.

The Brocken Spectre is quite unusual in the U.K., though not unknown especially in Scotland. It occurs when the sun shines strongly behind you as you look down into valley fog. The phenomena is in fact your own shadow massively enlarged by the depth of water droplets.

The 'hunchback' effect is particularly alarming, but it disappears when you remove your rucksack. The 'halo' is caused by refraction of light and is properly called a 'glory'. One odd thing is that you can only ever see the 'glory' of your own shadow.

Even the idea that the Deugar can lure people to their doom over the edges a a crag could be explained by the Brocken Spectre. The theory is that inexperienced hikers follow their own shadows into the mist, become disorientated, and they are not careful enough about where they are putting their feet...

Deugar or Brocken Spectre? Whichever explanation you prefer there is still a serious health warning. The Simonside Moors may look innocent enough on a warm summer's day, but conditions can change rapidly and peat bogs provide a very real hazard. Boots are strongly recommended and a sturdy stick will provide a measure of insurance against adders.

Deugars provide less of a threat as they are rarely seen during daylight hours - apart from dawn and at dusk.

Further mysteries are hidden is the grouse moor below the road. Here, hidden in the bracken, is the Iron Age fortress of Lordenshaws and fine examples of cup and ring marking.

Another Folly

The ramparts of Rothley are as artificial as the lakes - not that the coots and swans seem to mind. The gateway at the brow of the hill provides access to Codger Fort. This was the work of Capability Brown.

Original plans at Wallington show is was intended to complete the fort with a tower, flanking walls, and a bastion. It is now a film-set castle - impressive from the road, but with an empty lot behind it.

The Rothley Folly

To the south on Rothley Crags is another mock castle. A stile in a high wall leads to this unusual monument. The 'castle' is set above the huge rocks of the crags. It is a Camelot of an adventure playground, again unfinished, but with the feel of the real thing. A stone carved with a love-heart and the legend 'Bri luvs Trace' evokes a more recent age of folly.

The road to Hartington circles Gallows Hill. This is an impressive rolling landscape with fine old larches and beech coppices.

Hartington Hall has associations with Meg O'Meldon. By all accounts Meg was a plain girl, but wealthy father ensured that she found a suitable husband - Sir William Fenwick of Wallington.

Meg O'Meldon - A Mobile Phantom

Sir William died prematurely so Meg set about the serious business of becoming filthy rich. She transported huge quantities of coin and gold plate between her properties at Hartington and Meldon. It is said there was an underground passage constructed between the two houses (about twelve miles) so that she could distribute her wealth unobserved.

This may be as unlikely as efficient Channel Tunnel rail links, but there are still stories of undiscovered treasure. Meg's ghost, unable to rest until all the treasures are recovered, has been seen at Hartingdon, Meldon, and at

Newminster Abbey where she is buried. She is reputed to be the first upwardly mobile phantom.

The plantations of the Harwood Forest soften a bleak landscape on the approach to the Elsdon Gibbet. The carved head hanging from a wooden gallows is a vivid reminder of a celebrated crime.

Murder at the Raw

It began when the body of an elderly lady was found by a neighbour. The Elsdon Parish record for September Ist. 1791 simply reads : 'Margaret Crocer of the Raw murthered at do.'

The murder had taken place two days earlier at Raw Pele, a tower two miles to the north of Elsdon. The remote tower was situation on a well known 'travellers' way' - a route favoured by gypsies and pedlars who sought to avoid the turnpike charges.

Margaret (or 'Meg') Crozier ran a small shop which sold drapery and other goods. One consignment had recently arrived from Newcastle.

When a regular customer, Barbara Drummond, arrived at the shop she saw thread lying outside the closed doors. The circumstances were unusual enough for Barbara to seek out neighbours and voice her concern. Finally she entered the building with two of them, Elizabeth Jackson and William Dodds.

The door was unbolted and it was immediately clear that a great deal of material had been taken. On the first floor a door had been forced open and Margaret was found on her bed. A handkerchief had been tightly tied around her mouth and her hands were badly bruised. The cause of death was as obvious as it was horrific. Margaret Crozier's throat had been cut. The blood-stained knife was found later amongst the bedclothes.

William Winter, a member of a notorious family of robbers, was arrested on strong evidence which included eye witness reports that he was the owner of the knife. He was taken to Newcastle with two women accomplices. Their guilt in this crime was never seriously disputed. They were convicted together and executed outside the Westgate of the town on August 10th. 1792.

Winter showed great courage throughout the 16 hour trial and even carried one of the women who fell into a faint when the sentence was read. Eye witness accounts say that he mounted the scaffold on August 10th. 1792 with dignity.

Almost half an hour elapsed before the anguished twists and jerks at the end of the rope subsided, and ten minutes more were demanded by the executioner before the body was taken down.

Those who saw the corpse's face were horrified by the mutilation that the death agonies had caused to his once handsome features. The eyes were standing out from their sockets, and the tongue was blue and part severed by the victims own teeth. The skin was chaffed, blackened, and pitted around the forehead and mouth.

The Elsdon Gibbet

A popular picnic spot

The women were taken for dissection at Surgeons' Hall, but the strength of local feeling was such that Winter's body was brought back to Elsdon in a cart to be hung in chains at the specially constructed gibbet.

Near to the socket stone of the old Steng Cross, at the highest point of the old Morpeth to Elsdon turnpike, a 30 foot post was erected with a strong cross piece from which the corpse was to be hung. A special crane from the Carrick coal pit was used to hoist the already putrefying corpse in it iron cage into the hanging position. This was still the height of a famously warm summer and the stench, even from the ground, was said to be horrendous.

The body remained hanging in its own clothes until they rotted. It was then taken down, encased in a tarred sack, and replaced on the gibbet. What was finally removed from the site was described as a shrivelled mass of blackened filth and slime.

This edifying spectacle attracted sightseers from miles around and has been regarded by some as an early initiative to promote tourism in the area. To this day the gibbet is a popular picnic spot though all that hangs there now is a carved head.

It is enough to make you gasp a little when it is finally picked out by the beam of a torch on a dark night. This is a cold bleak place, even in summer. 200 years after the crime it is still not somewhere to be visited by people of a nervous disposition.

A Ghostly Encounter

There are many accounts suggesting that Winter's ghost still haunts the woods nearby. Tom Ebley, a visitor in the autumn of 1931, wrote :

" *I was taken by the chill of the wind and the way the clouds acted like a blind to the moonlight. The head rattled in its mounts and the flickering shadows played upon it. I had heard the tales of Winter's walking and now it seemed the putrid green flesh, rusted chains, and a knife that drips blood - gripped firmly in the skeletal fingers of the right hand - were no phantasms of the mind.* "

" *I heard a sound like groaning in the woods behind followed by a distinctive shuffling of feet. I dared not look in that direction but began to move away. The steps followed my course and I began to run. I reached my (motor) bike and started her up. As I moved off hastily I could hear a rattling of chains and a wild bark of laughter. I will not return to that place again.*"

The ghost of the murdered woman, Meg Crozier, is altogether more benign. The Hall family who farm today at the Raw are hardened to tales of Meg's moonlight wanderings around the farm buildings.

Whenever a door or window rattles in the darkness they say - 'That's either the breeze or Meg Crozier's ghostly hand.' Such is the the practical down-to-earth approach of the Northumberland farmer.

The Boot in the Fireplace

The descent into Elsdon provides almost an airplane window view of the Motte and Bailey Castle.

Elsdon is one of those villages you everybody seems to like. There is a nice uneven symmetry to it - all laid out around the village green. The Bird in the Bush is a traditional sort of hostelry that welcomes guests on bicycles or foot, as much as those in B.M.W's. The food is as highly recommended as the uniquely spooky atmosphere in which it can be enjoyed.

Walter and Linda Parker, the licensees, tell of a strange phenomenon that first began to manifest itself after building work had been carried out.

A wall and chimney were removed in 1961, some 180 years after the inn had been built. In the unblocked chimney area a child's boot was found. Walter believes that the boot was put in place to ward off evil. There is a minature horseshoe on the heel and iron nails protrude from the sole.

Allowing for the increased stature of modern youngsters It has been estimated that the boot belonged to a child of roughly ten years. It is kept behind the bar so the visitor can draw his own conclusions.

Walter tells of a wide range of poltergeist activity. Doors have mysteriously locked themselves. People have suffered digs in the ribs from unseen hands. Beer pumps have switched themselves off automatically. One particular armchair will rattle of its own accord and whicker baskets fly mysteriously off shelves.

An R.A.F. Officer staying at the inn found his lighter and cigarettes missing. A thorough search failed to find them until he again checked the table top where they had originally been placed.

The inn suffers from a mysterious opening and closing of doors when nobody is around, and visitors have said they have felt the force of some unseen presence.

Walter shrugs his shoulders and accepts it all philosophically. The Parkers have learned to live with their ghostly companion. They have no doubt who the culprit is.

" *It's the owner of the boot,* " says Walter.

Carvings in the Churchyard

Elsdon churchyard provides symbolic proof of past superstitions. You will find fine examples of the grim reaper and the death's head lovingly carved on tombstones.

The Churchyard at Elsdon

From Billsmoor to Holystone

The stark bleakness of Billsmoor is another face of the Northumberland countryside. If Coquetdale is Switzerland, then is Billsmoor is Siberia. Emily Bronte would have loved it, as do most of the residents. They are well-equipped for the climate - with woollen coats and four legs.

When you pass the impressive Holystone Grange it is obvious that this is the sort of building that deserves a decent ghost - a white lady at least. Sadly there are no records of hauntings.

The Salmon and the Ghostly Cavalier

However, the Salmon Inn though in Holystone village should be awarded a special rosette by The Good Ghost Guide.You will certainly get more than you bargain for if you order spirits here.

John and Sylvia Gilbertson, the proprietors, have become used to living with their ghostly guests. These include a mischievous poltergeist who borrows their belongings, a cavalier who's footsteps are heard echoing on the stairs, and a silent nun who keeps a lonely vigil.

It is the poltergeist that causes the most concern. Scissors have vanished from one room and have turned up inexplicably in another. Keys disappear from the ancient locks only to return days later. A caravan key seemed to be lost forever, only to reappear back on its appointed hook.

It was when a convalescent uncle woke up one morning to find a ghostly nun sitting at the bottom of his bed, that John and Sylvia began to take the idea of the haunted inn seriously. The uncle could not have known that the nearby woodyard was the site of a priory for Augustinian nuns who fled in terror from Scottish raids in 1322.

The nun has been seen before in Holystone, keeping a silent watch by the bed of a sick person.

Then there is the phantom cavalier.

Holystone, tucked away between wooded hills and the Coquet River, was a thriving royalist community in the Civil War. It is said that the cavalier took refuge in the priesthole at the Salmon Inn. Tradition has it he became too great a danger to the inn's proprietor who let him starve to death rather than risk the prying eyes of Cromwellian agents.

People will tell you that he walks abroad, shrouded safely by the darkest nights. John and Sylvia have never seen him, but they feel his presence particularly in one room. They have often heard footsteps on the stairs and landing when they know full well there is not living creature, other than themselves, in the building.

Even a 'ghostbusters team' from Rothbury failed to get close to the ghostly cavalier.

Ancient Rites at the Drakestone

It is worth the diversion to Harbottle to enjoy the twenty minute walk to the Drakestone.

The stone itself is associated with ancient druidical rites and there are rumours that blood sacrifices were a feature of these ceremonies. In more recent times children were passed over the stone as a remedy for minor ailments.

As a vantage point the Drakestone is superb. The village of Harbottle nestles like a contented cat in the valley. The proud ruins of the medieval castle are suspended precariously above the rooftops.

The twentieth century is still only a rumour in Harbottle.

The Phantom of Thropton

The road to Thropton is a delight to travel. The lushness and variety of the landscape must be seen to be believed. There is no finer English countryside.

The Thropton Phantom is as mysterious as any encountered in this journey.

A gravestone, set in the wall of a council house (2, The Meadows), is inscribed - 'John Green of Thropton died April 11th. 1731.' It is likely that the tombstone was moved somewhere close to its present site in 1850 when part of the churchyard at Rothbury was levelled.

This land was once part of John Green's farm. In 1935, when the council houses were built this singular headstone was incorporated into a wall.

But what of the man himself?

It is claimed that he murdered a priest and then committed suicide, thus making doubly sure that he could not be buried in consecrated ground.

The story makes little sense. Ninety-two years seems a rather advanced age for either murder or suicide. The suicide could not have occurred earlier, and the murder is not recorded. If it was a real event, what happened to the process of law? The authorities may have turned a blind eye to a few illicit stills, but not a murder surely?

Whatever the truth is we may never know. It is true to say however that there are serious claims that his ghost walks - often as a portent of misfortune. The spectre has been described as being tall, with angular features and short cropped hair. He wears a high collar.

Lord Armstrong - A Victorian Genius

A visit to the Cragside House and Estate at Rothbury is highly recommended. To enjoy the charm and beauty of Cragside you should make more than a fleeting visit and it is therefore not included in the itinerary of this tour.

Cragside, now in the care of the National Trust, is the classic creation of a Victorian genius, Lord Armstrong. The house is a model of practicability and style harnessed in harmony. The planting of seven million shrubs and trees was the cornerstone of a massive and spectacular landscaping scene.

As a tourist attraction Cragside comes in the 'not to be missed' category, but for a ghost-hunter, it is a disappointment. Indeed, it could almost be described as a ghost free zone.

It is true there is Nelly's Moss, a lake that has somehow become associated with a witch's 'trial by water'. The 'witch' - poor Nelly - allegedly met her end in those murky waters. The lake is for the most part artificial, and the story sounds as distorted as the early gramophones developed around the same time. Equally difficult to accept are stories of spectral children who are said to glide above the waters of Tumbleton lake. There are no records of drownings or disappearances, and perhaps the only real mystery of the lake is how it is kept so well stocked with fat rainbow trout.

In Rothbury itself it is recommended that you shake off the dust of your journey at the Coquet Vale Hotel. Here you will find a final phenomenon to consider.

A Fertility Chair

This friendly hotel is noted not only for fine food but also for a famous fertility chair located in the upstairs bar. The origins of the chair are obscure, but it has been at the hotel for as long as anyone can remember.

It is ornately carved with snakes, demons and dragons.

There have been many reports of miserable childless women who have been happily knitting bootees within weeks of sitting in the chair. One recent visitor from Lancashire claimed that it had performed its magic twice.

Lady visitors should therefore be warned. At the end of a day's ghosthunting you should avoid the chair at all costs - unless you hope to take home a permanent souvenir of your visit.

The Parish Church, Rothbury

Historical Notes

A number of important sites and personages are referred to only in passing in the main body of the text. These notes are intended to remedy that omission for those seeking greater clarification of historical contexts.

The information is arranged alphabetically.

8TH. EARL OF ARGYLL, ARCHIBALD CAMPBELL (1607-61) At one time the most powerful man in Scotland with a personal army of 20,000 retainers. He refused to be won over to the cause of Charles I and even courageously warned the King about his despotic ecclesiastical policy. In 1644, during the Civil War (qv) , he brought a Scottish army into England but was forced to return to suppress a royalist rising in the north. The horror in Scotland in 1649 at the news of the King's execution changed the political situation. In 1651 Argyll placed the crown on the head of the future Charles II at Scone, but was forced to submit to a Commonwealth army the following year after holding out at the besieged Inverary Castle for 11 months. This completed his political downfall. In 1660 he was arrested and found guilty of collaboration with Cromwellian forces and complicity in the death of Charles I. He was beheaded on the 27th. May 1661 before the warrant of execution had been signed.

'CAPABILITY' BROWN, LAUNCELOT (1715 - 83) English landscape gardener who revolutionised garden and parkland layout in the 1700's. He designed or remodelled nearly 150 estates including the gardens at Blenheim and Kew. He worked to achieve casual effects, with scatted groups of trees and gently rolling hills. He earned his nickname from a habit of saying that a place was 'capable of improvement'.

CATESBY, ROBERT (1573 - 1605) One of the leaders of the gunpowder plot to blow up King James I and his parliament. The conspirators were informed upon, and Guy Fawkes was discovered with gunpowder in a cellar of the Palace of Westminster. Catesby was killed while resisting arrest and Guy Fawkes was later executed.

CIVIL WAR, THE ENGLISH (1642 - 1651) More properly called the Civil Wars. The culmination of the deterioration in the relationship between the crown and the parliament through the reigns of James I and Charles I, and the financial and religious policies of Charles in particular, triggered rebellion in Scotland and Ireland. The short and long parliaments of 1640 demanded reform which included parliamentary control over the king's choice of advisors. In January 1642 Charles failed to secure the arrest of five members of parliament and quit the capital. He set up his standard at Nottingham in August of the same year. The royalists enjoyed early success in battles at Edgehill, Newcastle and Hopton, but failed to consolidate these victories. Scottish troops under Argyll (qv) entered England and contributed to the first parliamentary success at Marston Moor. Argyll's troops were withdrawn to deal with a royalist uprising in Scotland and an indecisive battle was fought at Newbury. In 1645 Fairfax's New Model Army inflicted a major defeat on the royalists at Naseby. In 1648 revolts in the south anticipated further intervention by the Scots on the king's behalf. Fairfax crushed the rebellion in the south and Cromwell defeated the invading Scots at Preston. Charles was tried by a court set up by the Rump Parliament and executed on 30th. January 1649. In 1650 Cromwell (qv) inflicted a final defeat on the Scots at Dunbar, and in the following year Charles II's invading army was crushed at Worcester. The Commonwealth formed to govern the country at the end of the war lasted until Booth's Rising and the Restoration of 1660.

COLLINGWOOD, CUTHBERT, Ist BARON (1759-1810) born in Newcastle upon Tyne, he joined the navy at the age of 11 and rose to the rank of Admiral. He fought outstandingly during the Napoleonic Wars and took over from Nelson after the latter's death at Trafalgar.

CORBRIDGE A much visited Roman site (Corstopitum) on the Stanegate. A fort and supply base which features an excellent museum.

CROMWELL, OLIVER (1599 - 1658) Represented Huntingdon in the parliament of 1628 and Cambridge in the Short and Long Parliaments. He was 43 at the outbreak of the Civil War and in three years rose from the rank of captain to lieutenant-general. He created and moulded a superb cavalry force and replaced Fairfax as lord-general in 1650. He defended the Commonwealth at Dunbar and Worcester and became Lord Protector and Head of State on 1653. Despite his reforming zeal and expert military leadership, Oliver Cromwell is best remembered as the prime mover in the trial and execution of King Charles I.

DUNBAR, BATTLE OF (3rd. September 1650) Cromwell (qv) surprised the Scots with a dawn attack. David Leslie's army was utterly routed and prisoners were taken to Alnwick where many died of starvation.

EDWARD THE CONFESSOR, SAINT (King of England 1042 - 66. Canonized 1161) Edward drove his greatest rival, Godwin, in exile (1051) and recognised his Norman cousin, William the Conqueror, as his successor. On Godwin's death, Harold Godwinson (qv) (later King Harold II) became the leading influence in the country. Edward contented himself with piety and good works which included the building of Westminster Abbey.

EDWARD II (1307 - 1327. Born 1284) Edward's reign was punctuated by famine, failures in war and baronial opposition. His extravagance and homosexuality made him unpopular, but the murder of a favourite (Gaveston) in 1312 destroyed the united face of the opposition. He suffered humiliating defeats at Bannockburn and in France and new opposition grew around Roger and Isabella Mortimer. Edward was deposed and brutally murdered in September 1327.

EDWARD IV (1461 - 1470, 1471 - 83. Born 1442.) A brave and popular soldier during the Wars of the Roses (qv). He won a significant victory at Towton (1461), but his marriage to Elizabeth Woodville alienated his mentor, Warwick the Kingmaker. He was driven into exile but returned to lead a sucessful campaign in March 1471. He gave England domestic peace but failed to reconcile disputes at court. The most important of these, between the Woodvilles and the Duke of Gloucester (the future Richard III) caused further strife after his death.

EDWARD VII (King of England 1901 - 10. Born 1481) Queen Victoria's heir who was largely cut off from political influence until his succession. Edward was a notorious womaniser who also over indulged in food, gambling and shooting. He was an affable and generally popular monarch.

ELIZABETH 1 (Queen of England 1558 - 1603. Born 1533) In 1536 her mother, Anne Boleyn, was executed in the Tower on the order of her father, Henry V111. Elizabeth herself was imprisoned in the Tower during the reign of her half-sister, Mary. Her political astuteness helped her not only to survive, but to become one of England's most celebrated monarchs. Her reign brought peace, and a measure of religious settlement until the War with Spain in 1585. The scuttling of the Armada settled that conflict, but revolts in Ireland and the Earl of Essex's rebellion were symptoms of unresolved difficulties. These seeds of discontent culminated in Civil War of 1642 and the end of absolute monarchy in Britain.

ERIC BLOODAXE, KING OF NORTHUMBRIA (Died 954) A son of Harald Finehair, King of Norway, Eric was born, and possibly died, a pagan. Yet one cleric, Archbishop Wulfstan, had joined with other notables of the day to make him king and another wrote sympathetically of his death at Stainmore, following treachery. It is certain, too, that sometime between 952 and his death he visited Cuthbert's shrine. He was king twice. Once, for possibly only a few months around 947 and then again from 951 to 954. A strong ruler and warrior, he also appears to have been well liked and would undoubtedly be at the head of any 'Home Rule for Northumbria' movement, were he alive today.

FLODDEN, BATTLE OF (9th. September 1513) The army of Scotland's James 1V was out-manoeuvred and defeated by the Earl of Surrey. English casualties were relatively light, but the Scots lost over 10,000 men. The Archbishop of St. Andrews and King James himself were numbered amongst the slain.

GAUNT, JOHN OF (1340 - 1399) Duke of Lancaster and third son of Edward III. A prime political mover of his day with some influence over Richard II (qv). His eldest son became Henry 1V and among his descendants are Edward IV (qv), Henry VII, Mary, Queen of Scots, Warwick the Kingmaker (qv) and Henry Beaufort, Duke of Somerset, confidant of Margaret of Anjou (qv).

HAROLD II (King of England 1066. Born c. 1022) Harold Godwinson was elected king on Edward the Confessor's death. Scored a famous victory over Harold Hardrada at Stamford Bridge (qv), but his weary army were defeated by the invading forces of William the Conqueror at Hastings.

HENRY V (King of England 1413 - 1422. Born 1387) The first king to be fully literate in English. He claimed the French throne and embarked with an expeditionary force across the channel. He marched on Calais and won a famous victory at Agincourt in 1415. After diplomatic manoeuvring, he advanced through Normandy capturing Caen, Falaise and Rouen. After forming an important political alliance with Armagnac he carried on his triumph at Troyes (1420). He contracted dysentery during the siege at Meaux and died on 31st. August 1422 at the age of 35.

HENRY VI (1422 - 1461, 1470 - 71. Born 1421) Succeeded to the thrones of England and France before his first birthday. He came of age in 1456 but showed little inclination for ruling. He was dominated by the Duke of Suffolk and his wife, Margaret of Anjou (qv). His decline into insanity precipitated the Wars of the Roses (qv). On his restoration he became a pawn of Warwick the Kingmaker (qv). After Warwick's fall Henry was captured at Barnet, confined to the Tower, and murdered on the orders of King Edward IV (qv).

HENRY VIII (1509 - 47. Born 1491) Henry came to the throne with little political or governmental experience. He learned these skills quickly and presided over one of the most lavish and cultured courts in Europe. His decision to divorce Catherine of Aragon created a division with Rome and the establishment of the Church of England. He was always the final power in government but had little taste for administration. This was left to famous servants, notably the three Thomas' - More, Cromwell, and Wolsey (qv) - all of whom suffered considerably after falling from the king's favour. Henry is now best remembered for his six wives and as the composer of Greensleeves.

HEXHAM, BATTLES OF (1463 and 1464) It was after the first of these battles during the Wars of the Roses (qv) that Margaret of Anjou (qv) hid with her son. She was later to escape to France.

HOTSPUR, SIR HENRY PERCY. (1364 - 1403) Son of the Earl of Northumberland, Hotspur was particularly zealous in guarding the borders. Captured by the Scots at Otterburn (qv) (1388), he later helped Henry IV to the throne, won a victory for him at Homildon Hill (1402), but changed sides and died at the Battle of Shrewsbury (qv) (1403). Hotspur, who has near legendary status in Northumberland, was portrayed as a contemporary of Prince Henry (later Henry V (qv)) by Shakespeare. He was in fact 23 years older than the prince. But the near sibling rivalry between the two 'young men' is an important theme in Henry IV Part One. Shakespeare climaxes the play with Prince Hal locked in mortal combat with Hotspur on the battlefield. The fatal blow provokes the words - ' Oh Harry! Thou hast robbed me of my youth. 'Hotspur was killed a few months before his 40th. birthday.

HOUSESTEADS draws more visitors than any of the other wall forts. This is mainly due to its fine elevated position on the Whin Sill crags. In the settlement there are remains of houses and shops, but this was basically a large fort (Borcovicium or Vercovicium) which held a garrison of around 1000 men. The nearby museum contains plans and models of the fort as well as sculpted stone and pottery. The whole area is in the care of the Department of the Environment.

JACOBITES is the name given to the supporters of the deposed James II (VII of Scotland) and his son, James. Jacobite plots began in 1688, but the first serious threat to the Hanoverian succession came in 1715. This was the Earl of Mar's Scottish rising, which was supported by Northumberland's Thomas Forster and the Earl of Derwentwater. The rebels reached Preston where they capitulated. The more serious affair was in 1745. 'Bonnie Prince

Charlie' had landed in Scotland two years previously with 10,000 French troops. The standard was raised at Glenfinnan in '45 and support came mainly from the west and central highlands. The prince captured Perth and Edinburgh, and a victory at Prestonpans encouraged him to march into the heart of England. The expected support did not materialise and the prince turned back at Derby. There was a last victory at Falkirk before the slaughter of the highlanders at Culloden Moor. Prince Charles escaped with his life, but the Jacobite cause was lost.

JAMES II and VII (King of Great Britain 1685 - 1688. Born 1633.) James was a capable soldier and sailor but an inept politician. He survived the Exclusion Crisis after his conversion to Catholicism, but was deposed when his efforts to recatholicize England provoked the Glorious Revolution.

JONES, INIGO (1573 - 1652) An English architect who became the king's surveyor of works in 1615. He imported Italian Palladio styles into England. The Royal Banqueting Hall in Whitehall, London, is considered to be his masterpiece.

LUTYENS, SIR EDWIN (1869 - 1944) A British architect, often described as 'the last English designer of country houses'.

MARGARET OF ANJOU (1430 - 1482) Daughter of the King of Naples who was betrothed to King Henry VI (qv) at the age of 14 and married in England the following year. A key player on the Lancastrian team during the Wars of the Roses (qv), especially during the period of her husband's insanity. She was forced to flea for her safety twice - to Scotland in 1460 and 1461. In the following year her forces were overwhelmed by a storm at sea and she escaped in an open boat to Berwick. By 1463 she was again trying to raid the Northumberland coast and met with many hardships and adventures. On one occasion she escaped capture by the generosity of a Yorkist squire who carried her off on his own horse. Finally she and her son were brought to Bamburgh through the compassion of a robber they had encountered in the forest. In August she escaped to Flanders before returning to the protection of her father in France. Seven years later she took advantage of the quarrel between the Earl of Warwick (qv) and King Edward 1V (qv) to return. Margaret landed at Weymouth on the day of Warwick's defeat at Barnet. Three weeks later the Lancastrians were defeated at Tewkesbury. Her only son, Edward, was killed in the battle. This time there was no escape. Margaret was arrested and taken to London where she was held prisoner for five years. In 1476 she was ransomed by the French King, Louis X11, and lived on a modest pension until her death in April 1482. She was buried in Angers Cathedral. Margaret of Anjou is remembered not just as a warrior queen, but as an attractive, determined and intelligent lady. There are unsubstantiated romantic links with William de la Pole, Earl of Suffolk, and Henry Beaufort, Duke of Somerset. The first of these relationships was a matter of much speculation and scandal at the time.

OSWALD, KING OF NORTHUMBRIA (circa 605 - 642) Exiled by his uncle, he is known to have spent some time on Iona. He became King by defeating the British King Cadwalla near Chollerford in 634. He sent for a Bishop and on the arrival of Aidan, gave him Lindisfarne and the royal city of Bamburgh. He completed the building of York Minster begun by his uncle, but was finally killed in battle.

OTTERBURN, BATTLE OF (5th August 1388) Scots raiding party under James, Earl of Douglas were attacked by Hotspur (qv) at dusk. Douglas was killed, Hotspur taken prisoner and victory claimed by the Scots. Also known as 'The Battle by Moonlight' and 'Chevy Chase'.

PRINCES IN THE TOWER (disappeared 1485) Edward V and his brother Richard, Duke of York were the sons of Edward IV (qv). Declared illegitimate, the throne was taken by Richard, Duke of Gloucester (later Richard III (qv)) at the death of Edward IV. Shakespeare and most popular histories has them murdered by order of Richard III, though they actually posed a much greater threat to his successor, Henry VII.

RICHARD I, 'THE LIONHEART' (1189 - 1199. Born 1157) A son of Henry II, he spent only 6 months of his reign in England, preferring his French castles when he wasn't away at the Crusades. His brother, John, was Regent in his absence and tried to take the throne for himself.

RICHARD II (1377 - 1399. Born 1367) Began as a successful king, probably under the guidance of his uncle, John of Gaunt (qv). Lost control for a while to the 'Merciless Parliament'. Later became tyrannical, banishing Henry Bolingbroke (later King Henry IV) among other apparently senseless acts. Was probably murdered in Pontefract Castle.

RICHARD III (1483 - 1485. Born 1452) Gained fame, but never popularity, as a soldier whilst his brother, Edward IV (qv) was king. Shakespeare has him portrayed as a hunchbacked monster, responsible for the murder of the Princes in the Tower (qv). There is no evidence that he was hunchbacked, but it was certainly politically expedient for Henry VII to have him maligned.

RIDLEY, NICHOLAS (circa 1500 - 1555) Born in Northumberland, chaplain to Archbishop Cranmer and later Bishop of London, Ridley was an energetic Protestant and did much to further the cause of the Reformation. He was burned at the stake alongside Bishop Latimer.

ROSES, WARS OF THE (1455-1487) This is perhaps a rather grandiose title for intermittent fighting, lasting no more than 13 weeks in total, during which the crown of England changed hands 6 times. It began during the reign of Henry VI (qv), whilst he was mentally incapable of ruling. Control was sought by the Lancastrian, or Court Party under Henry's wife, Margaret of Anjou (qv) supported by the Beauforts and the Yorkists led by Richard, Duke of York. They ended when the Lancastrian claimant to the throne, Henry VII married the eldest daughter of Edward IV (qv) a Yorkist king

SHREWSBURY, BATTLE OF (21st July, 1403) Henry IV attacked Hotspur's (qv) rebel army before reinforcements could reach it. Hotspur was killed.

STAMFORD BRIDGE, BATTLE OF (25th September 1066) Fought by Harold Godwinson (qv) against Harald Hardrada and his ally Godwinson's brother, Tostig (qv). Harold Godwinson won, but his army were weakened after their forced march north to York. The second forced march, to meet the Normans near Hastings contributed to the defeat.

STANEGATE was an important supply road for Hadrian's Wall. It runs from west of Carlisle via Vindolanda (qv) to Corbridge, where it links with a contemporary road, Dere Street, which was also built by Agricola.

TOSTIG (died 1066) Brother of King Harold (qv) and Earl of Northumbria, he provoked a revolt against Harold in Northumbria in 1065 and was exiled. He returned in 1066, bringing an army with him, only to die at Stamford Bridge (qv).

WARWICK, RICHARD NEVILLE, EARL OF, 'THE KINGMAKER' (1428-1471) Great statesman and soldier of the period. Sided initially with the Yorkists during the Wars of the Roses (qv), his capture of Henry VI (qv) helped put Edward IV (qv) on the throne, behind which Richard Neville was definitely the power. Losing influence and power, he changed sides, helping Henry VI back to the throne. He was killed at the Battle of Barnet.

WILLIAM II (1087 - 1100. Born 1056) Brutal, ruthless king who quelled two uprisings, humbled the Welsh and Scots and was murdered (probably) on the orders of his brother, later Henry I.

WILLIAM THE LION, KING OF SCOTLAND (1165 - 1214. Born 1143) A younger brother of Malcolm IV, he joined the alliance against Henry II, but his invasion led only to his capture at Alnwick in 1174. He bought a pardon from Richard I (qv), then failed ignominiously to wrest the borders from John.

WOLSEY, Thomas, Cardinal (1475 - 1530) Effectively England's chief administrator as Henry V111's (qv) chancellor (1515 - 1529). A man of outstanding ability who fell from grace after failing to persuade the pope to allow Henry to divorce Catherine of Aragon. He died on his way to face trial in London.

VANBRUGH, SIR JOHN (1664 - 1726) England's most successful baroque architect. Seaton Delaval Hall, Blenheim Palace and Castle Howard are claimed to be his finest pieces.

VINDOLANDA was a Roman civilian settlement to the south of Hadrian's Wall and pre-dating it by about forty years. It was originally built as part of a defence line to guard the Stanegate (qv). The remains of the headquarters building are said to be the finest of their kind in the country.

Illusion of the empty lot.
(See page 84) 'Another Folly'